I0606389

Biscuits
& Quick Breads

83 press®

83 Press
2323 2nd Avenue North
Birmingham, Alabama 35203
83press.com

ISBN 979-8-9923853-9-7
Printed in China

Contributing Recipe Development
Kellie Gerber Kelley

Contributing Food Stylists
Kellie Gerber Kelley, Erin Merhar

Contributing Photographers
Beau Gustafson, Alison Miksch

Biscuits & Quick Breads

Everyday Comfort Done Right

from the HOFFMAN MEDIA TEST KITCHEN

CONTENTS

Introduction

Welcome to *Biscuits & Quick Breads*! We hope this book helps you add some magic to your meals.

Some days—even the busy ones when you're short on time—call for something homemade and comforting hot out of the oven. These pages are filled with lots of sweet and savory ideas that satisfy the craving but don't take a lot of time or effort.

You'll find options for breakfasts that are quick enough to make on a weekday and others that are ideal for weekends. There are also hearty entrées, standout side dishes, and memorable desserts that could easily become part of your weekly rotation.

With this book in hand, you'll want to gather around the table.

Classic Tastes

There are some biscuits and quick breads that stand the test of time. This chapter shares well-loved recipes that will hopefully become favorites in your home.

Drop Biscuits

MAKES 11

This recipe is a breezy wonder, with craggy peaked tops that offer a bit of crunch paired with the signature soft interior. The final brush with butter? Consider that its brush with greatness.

½ cup cold unsalted butter
1¾ cups all-purpose flour
1½ cups cake flour
2 tablespoons sugar
1 tablespoon baking powder
1 teaspoon kosher salt
1¾ cups whole buttermilk, chilled
2 tablespoons salted butter, melted
Honey, to serve

1. Preheat oven to 400°. Line a baking sheet with parchment paper.

2. Using a bench scraper, cut cold unsalted butter into cubes, and freeze until ready to use.

3. In a large bowl, stir together flours, sugar, baking powder, and salt. Place three-fourths of flour mixture in the work bowl of a food processor; add cold butter, and pulse until mixture is crumbly with some pea-size pieces of butter remaining. Return mixture to large bowl, and stir to combine with remaining flour mixture. (Alternatively, cut cold butter into flour mixture using a pastry blender or 2 forks.) Add cold buttermilk, stirring just until combined. (Dough will be sticky and wet.)

4. Using a ¼-cup measuring cup, scoop dough, and drop 2 inches apart onto prepared pan. Brush top of biscuits with half of melted, salted butter.

5. Bake for 8 minutes. Reduce oven temperature to 375°, and bake until golden brown, 8 to 10 minutes more. Remove from oven, and brush with remaining half of melted, salted butter. Serve hot with honey.

Cornmeal Drop Biscuits

MAKES 12

Soup lovers, take note—these are the biscuits for you! The perfect marriage of cornbread and biscuits, they're great for crumbling into your favorite hearty stews and soups. These biscuits come together quickly and easily. You can make them while your soup is simmering.

2 cups self-rising flour
½ cup stone-ground white cornmeal
⅔ cup cold unsalted butter, cubed
1 to 1¼ cups whole buttermilk

1. Preheat oven to 400°. Line a baking sheet with parchment paper.

2. In a large bowl, whisk together flour and cornmeal. Using a pastry blender or 2 forks, cut butter into flour mixture until crumbly. Make a well in flour mixture; add 1 cup buttermilk, stirring until mixture just comes together. (Add remaining ¼ cup buttermilk, if needed.)

3. Drop dough by 3 tablespoonfuls 1 inch apart on prepared pan.

4. Bake until golden brown, 12 to 14 minutes.

Cornmeal Cathead Biscuits and Tomato Shrimp Gravy

MAKES 5

Canned tomatoes make this gravy simple and accessible—even when tomatoes are out of season. It pairs wonderfully with the impressive yet almost effortless Cornmeal Cathead Biscuits.

CORNMEAL CATHEAD BISCUITS

3½ cups self-rising flour
1½ cups fine plain yellow cornmeal*
1 teaspoon kosher salt
½ cup cold unsalted butter, cubed
2 cups cold whole milk
1 large egg
1 teaspoon water

TOMATO-SHRIMP GRAVY
Makes 5 servings

3 tablespoons bacon drippings
3 tablespoons all-purpose flour
1½ cups vegetable broth
½ pound medium fresh shrimp, peeled and deveined
1 (14.5-ounce) can diced tomatoes, undrained
1 teaspoon kosher salt
1 teaspoon ground black pepper
1 tablespoon chopped fresh parsley
Cornmeal Cathead Biscuits, to serve (recipe follows)
Garnish: chopped fresh parsley, chopped cooked bacon

For the Biscuits:

1. Preheat oven to 375°. Spray a 12-inch cast-iron skillet with cooking spray.

2. In a large bowl, whisk together flour, cornmeal, and salt. Using a pastry blender or 2 forks, cut in cold butter until mixture is crumbly. Stir in cold milk with a fork until well combined. Scoop dough by about 1 cupful, and drop into prepared pan.

3. In a small bowl, whisk together egg with 1 teaspoon water; brush onto biscuits.

4. Bake until golden brown, about 35 minutes. Serve warm.

For the Gravy:

1. In a 10-inch cast-iron skillet, heat bacon drippings over medium heat. Whisk in flour until smooth; cook, whisking constantly, until pale brown, about 2 minutes. Gradually whisk in broth until smooth.

2. Stir in shrimp, tomatoes, salt, and pepper; cook, stirring occasionally, until thickened and shrimp are pink and firm, about 8 minutes. Stir in parsley. Serve immediately with Cornmeal Cathead Biscuits. Garnish with parsley and bacon, if desired.

**We used Goya Fine Yellow Corn Meal.*

Sweet Potato Drop Biscuits

MAKES 10

It's always a tough decision when making sweet potato biscuits—do you take them in a sweet or savory direction? These easy peppery drop biscuits are a savory win. Pair them with ham at Easter or with turkey at Thanksgiving, and they're always delicious on their own.

- **1½ cups self-rising flour**
- **¾ cup cooked mashed sweet potato**
- **6 tablespoons whole buttermilk**
- **6 tablespoons unsalted butter, melted and divided**
- **¼ teaspoon ground black pepper**

1. Preheat oven to 425°. Line a baking sheet with parchment paper.

2. Place flour in a medium bowl. In a small bowl, whisk together sweet potato, buttermilk, and 4 tablespoons melted butter. Make a well in flour; add sweet potato mixture, stirring until mixture just comes together. Drop biscuits by 3 tablespoonfuls 1 inch apart onto prepared pan.

3. Bake until lightly browned, about 10 minutes. Brush with remaining 2 tablespoons melted butter, and sprinkle with pepper. Bake until golden brown, about 5 minutes more. Let cool on a wire rack for 10 minutes.

Flaky Buttermilk Biscuits

MAKES ABOUT 12

Equally delicious slathered with jam and honey for breakfast, filled with meat and cheese for lunch, or brushed with garlic butter as a standout side dish for dinner, these classic biscuits with their buttery, flaky layers will become your go-to for every meal.

- 3½ cups all-purpose flour
- 2 tablespoons sugar
- 1 tablespoon kosher salt
- 1 tablespoon baking powder
- 1 cup cold unsalted butter, cubed
- 1 cup cold whole buttermilk

1. Preheat oven to 425°.
2. In a large bowl, whisk together flour, sugar, salt, and baking powder. Using a pastry blender or 2 forks, cut in cold butter until mixture is crumbly and butter is the size of peas. Using a fork, stir in cold buttermilk until a shaggy dough forms.
3. Turn out dough onto a lightly floured surface. Pat dough into a 10x8-inch rectangle, and cut into fourths. Stack pieces of dough on top of each other, and pat or roll into a rectangle again. Repeat process three more times. Pat or roll dough to ¾-inch thickness. Using a 2½-inch round cutter dipped in flour, cut dough without twisting cutter. Gently reroll and cut scraps once. Place biscuits on a parchment-lined baking sheet. Freeze until cold, about 10 minutes.
4. Place biscuits 1 inch apart on a cast-iron baking pan or the smooth side of a cast-iron griddle.
5. Bake until top is golden brown, 10 to 15 minutes. Serve warm with desired toppings.

Buttermilk Biscuits with Sausage Gravy

MAKES 10

Everyone needs to have a good buttermilk biscuit recipe under their belt. This is baking at its most basic!

- **2½ cups self-rising flour**
- **2 tablespoons sugar**
- **2¾ teaspoons kosher salt, divided**
- **¾ cup cold unsalted butter, cubed**
- **1 cup whole buttermilk, chilled**
- **2 tablespoons unsalted butter, melted**
- **1 (16-ounce) package ground pork sausage**
- **¼ cup all-purpose flour**
- **3 cups whole milk**
- **½ cup heavy whipping cream**
- **2 teaspoons apple cider vinegar**
- **⅛ teaspoon garlic powder**
- **⅛ teaspoon ground black pepper**

1. Preheat oven to 425°. Line a rimmed baking sheet with parchment paper. In a large bowl, whisk together flour, sugar, and 1¼ teaspoons salt. Using a pastry blender or 2 forks, cut cubed butter into flour mixture until crumbly. Make a well in flour mixture; add cold buttermilk, stirring until mixture just comes together.

2. Turn out dough onto a heavily floured surface. Shape dough into a flat log, and fold into thirds, like a letter. Roll into a 10x9-inch rectangle. Using a 3-inch round cutter dipped in flour, cut 10 biscuits, without twisting cutter; reroll scraps as necessary. Place biscuits 2 inches apart on prepared pan. Brush tops with melted butter.

3. Bake until golden brown, about 12 minutes.

4. In a large skillet, cook sausage over medium-high heat, stirring occasionally, until browned and crumbly, about 10 minutes. Sprinkle flour over sausage, stirring to coat. Gradually whisk in milk and cream. Stir in vinegar, 1½ teaspoons salt, garlic powder, and pepper. Bring to a simmer, whisking constantly, until thickened, about 10 minutes. Serve immediately over warm Buttermilk Biscuits.

Sweet Potato Biscuits

MAKES 10 TO 12

There's something about the warm orange glow of sweet potato biscuits that makes you smile. Toasted pecans stirred into the dough take them over the top.

- 2 cups all-purpose flour
- 2 tablespoons sugar
- 1 tablespoon baking powder
- ¾ teaspoon kosher salt
- ¼ teaspoon ground ginger
- ¼ teaspoon ground nutmeg
- ½ cup cold unsalted butter, cubed
- ⅓ cup toasted pecans, chopped
- 1 (15-ounce) can cut sweet potatoes in syrup,* drained well and coarsely mashed
- ¾ cup whole buttermilk, divided
- 1 tablespoon unsalted butter, melted
- Cane syrup, to serve

1. Preheat oven to 425°.

2. In a large bowl, whisk together flour, sugar, baking powder, salt, ginger, and nutmeg. Using a pastry blender or 2 forks, cut butter into flour mixture until crumbly. Make a well in flour mixture; add pecans, sweet potato, and ⅔ cup buttermilk, stirring until mixture just comes together. Add remaining buttermilk, if necessary. (Dough will be sticky.)

3. On a heavily floured surface, gently knead dough 4 or 5 times. Roll dough ¾ inch thick. Fold dough in half; roll ¾ inch thick. Using a 2½-inch round cutter dipped in flour, cut 10 to 12 biscuits, without twisting cutter, rerolling scraps once. Place biscuits in a 12-inch cast-iron skillet or on a parchment-lined baking sheet.

4. Bake until lightly browned, about 17 minutes. Brush with melted butter. Serve with cane syrup.

**We used Bruce's.*

Whole Wheat Biscuits

MAKES 12

Whole wheat flour gets a bad rap for making baked goods chewy. Solve the problem with a simple solution—add in some regular all-purpose flour. The result is a wholesome biscuit with a great tender texture.

1 cup all-purpose flour
1 cup whole wheat flour
5 teaspoons baking powder
1 tablespoon sugar
¾ teaspoon kosher salt
½ cup unsalted butter, cubed
1 cup plus 3 tablespoons whole buttermilk, divided
Honey, to serve

1. Preheat oven to 450°.

2. In a large bowl, whisk together flours, baking powder, sugar, and salt. Using a pastry blender or 2 forks, cut butter into flour mixture until crumbly. Make a well in flour mixture; add 1 cup buttermilk, stirring until mixture just comes together. (Add remaining 3 tablespoons buttermilk, if needed.)

3. Turn out dough onto a lightly floured surface and knead 2 to 3 times. Roll dough into an 8-inch circle. Using a 2-inch round cutter dipped in flour, cut 12 biscuits, without twisting cutter, rerolling scraps as necessary. Place biscuits 1 inch apart on an ungreased baking sheet.

4. Bake until golden brown, about 12 minutes. Let cool for 10 minutes before serving. Serve with honey.

Roll-Out Biscuits

MAKES 12

Take the formula for a roll-out buttermilk biscuit one step further and throw in a flaky twist. A quick brush with buttermilk and a trifold of the dough create light layers in this golden biscuit, making it perfect to split open and spread with jam.

- 1½ cups cold unsalted butter
- 2½ cups all-purpose flour
- 2½ cups cake flour
- ¼ cup sugar
- 3½ tablespoons baking powder
- 4 teaspoons kosher salt
- 2 cups plus 2 tablespoons whole buttermilk, chilled and divided
- 2 tablespoons salted butter, melted
- Jam, to serve

1. Line a baking sheet with parchment paper.
2. Using a bench scraper, cut cold unsalted butter into cubes, and freeze until ready to use.
3. In a large bowl, stir together flours, sugar, baking powder, and salt. Place three-fourths of flour mixture in the work bowl of a food processor; add cold butter, and pulse until mixture is crumbly with some pea-size pieces of butter remaining. Return mixture to large bowl, and stir to combine with remaining flour mixture. (Alternatively, cut cold butter into flour mixture using a pastry blender or 2 forks.) Add 2 cups cold buttermilk, stirring just until combined.
4. Turn out dough onto a heavily floured surface, and pat into a 15x6-inch rectangle. Brush dough with remaining 2 tablespoons cold buttermilk. Fold dough into thirds. Reflour work surface, and roll dough to 1-inch thickness. Using a 2½-inch round cutter dipped in flour, cut dough without twisting cutter. (Since this dough is laminated, it cannot be rerolled like normal roll-out biscuits. The rerolls will not match the final product from the first roll.) Place biscuits about ½ inch apart on prepared pan. Refrigerate for at least 30 minutes.
5. Preheat oven to 375°.
6. Brush top of biscuits with half of melted, salted butter, and bake until golden brown, 16 to 18 minutes. Remove from oven, and brush with remaining half of melted, salted butter. Serve hot with jam.

Lard Biscuits

MAKES ABOUT 10

When cutting lard into flour, the fat coats the flour particles and reduces gluten formation, which results in a very tender biscuit.

3 cups self-rising flour*
2 teaspoons kosher salt
1½ teaspoons sugar
¾ cup cold lard, cut into ½-inch cubes, plus more for greasing pan
1 cup cold whole buttermilk, plus more for brushing

1. Preheat oven to 425°. Line a baking sheet with parchment paper.

2. In a large bowl, whisk together flour, salt, and sugar. Using a pastry blender or 2 forks, cut in cold lard until the size of peas. Using a fork, stir in buttermilk until a shaggy dough forms.

3. Turn out dough onto a lightly floured surface; gently knead 4 times. Roll or pat dough to about 1¼-inch thickness. Using a 2¼-inch round cutter, cut dough, without twisting cutter; reroll and cut scraps. Place biscuits on prepared pan; freeze for 15 minutes.

4. Generously grease a 14-inch cast-iron baking pan with lard. Place pan in oven until very hot, about 5 minutes. Carefully place biscuits on hot pan; brush tops with buttermilk.

5. Bake until golden brown, 13 to 15 minutes. Let cool on pan for 10 minutes before serving.

**We used White Lily.*

Fried Buttermilk Biscuits

MAKES ABOUT 10

These crispy, sweet biscuits are a delicious blank canvas for all your favorite gravies.

- **2½ tablespoons vegetable oil, plus more for frying**
- **2½ cups self-rising flour**
- **¼ teaspoon kosher salt**
- **1¼ cups whole buttermilk**

1. In a large Dutch oven, pour oil to fill halfway full, and heat over medium heat until a deep-fry thermometer registers 350°.

2. In a medium bowl, whisk together flour and salt. Add buttermilk and remaining 2½ tablespoons oil, stirring until a thick batter forms.

3. Carefully drop batter by ¼ cupfuls into hot oil, avoiding overcrowding pan. Fry, turning occasionally, until golden brown, about 4 minutes. Remove using a slotted spoon, and let drain on paper towels. Serve warm.

Angel Biscuits

MAKES 11

A cross between a buttermilk biscuit and a Parker House roll, these Angel Biscuits will impress any and all at the dinner table. With its pillowy softness and golden buttery top, take one bite, and you'll never question its name again.

- **¼ cup all-vegetable shortening**
- **¼ cup cold unsalted butter**
- **2 tablespoons warm water (105° to 110°)**
- **1 teaspoon active dry yeast**
- **2 tablespoons sugar**
- **1½ cups all-purpose flour**
- **1¼ cups cake flour**
- **2 teaspoons kosher salt**
- **½ teaspoon baking powder**
- **¼ teaspoon baking soda**
- **1 cup whole buttermilk**
- **2 tablespoons salted butter, melted**

1. Using a bench scraper, cut shortening and cold unsalted butter into cubes, and freeze until ready to use.

2. In a small bowl, stir together 2 tablespoons warm water and yeast until yeast is dissolved. Stir in sugar, and let stand until mixture is foamy, about 5 minutes.

3. In a medium bowl, whisk together flours, salt, baking powder, and baking soda. Place three-fourths of flour mixture in the work bowl of a food processor; add cold shortening and cold butter, and pulse until mixture is crumbly with some pea-size pieces of butter remaining. Return mixture to large bowl, and stir to combine with remaining flour mixture. (Alternatively, cut cold shortening and cold butter into flour mixture using a pastry blender or 2 forks.) Add yeast mixture and buttermilk, stirring just until dry ingredients are moistened. Cover and refrigerate for 1 hour.

4. Line a baking sheet with parchment paper.

5. Turn out dough onto a lightly floured surface, and knead 4 or 5 times. Pat dough to ¾-inch thickness. Using a 2½-inch round cutter, cut dough, without twisting cutter, rerolling scraps only once. Place on prepared pan. Cover and let rise in a warm, draft-free place (75°) until puffed, about 1 hour.

6. Preheat oven to 375°.

7. Brush biscuits with melted, salted butter, and bake until golden brown, 12 to 15 minutes. Let cool on pan for 5 minutes. Serve warm.

Cornmeal Angel Biscuits

MAKES ABOUT 13

These heavenly biscuits are a dream. The instant yeast helps create the light and fluffy texture that these biscuits are known for.

4 cups all-purpose flour, divided
2 cups finely ground plain yellow cornmeal, divided
1 cup cold unsalted butter, cubed
¼ cup sugar
1 (0.25-ounce) package instant yeast
1½ tablespoons kosher salt
1 tablespoon baking powder
1 teaspoon baking soda
2 cups warm whole buttermilk (120° to 130°)
2 tablespoons cold whole buttermilk
Butter, to serve

1. In a large bowl, whisk together 2 cups flour and 1 cup cornmeal. Using a pastry blender or 2 forks, cut in cold butter until crumbly; refrigerate.

2. In another large bowl, whisk together sugar, yeast, salt, baking powder, baking soda, remaining 2 cups flour, and remaining 1 cup cornmeal. Stir in warm buttermilk until combined. Let mixture stand until cooled. Stir in refrigerated flour mixture until a dough forms. (Dough will be slightly sticky.)

3. Preheat oven to 400°. Spray a 12-inch cast-iron skillet with cooking spray.

4. Turn out dough onto a lightly floured surface. Pat dough into a 1-inch-thick rectangle; cut in half. Stack halves; press into a 1-inch-thick rectangle. Repeat process 3 more times, flouring surface as needed. Using a 2½-inch round cutter dipped in flour, cut dough, without twisting cutter. Reroll scraps once, and cut additional biscuits. Place biscuits about ½ inch apart in prepared pan. Cover and let stand in a warm, draft-free place (75°) until puffed, 30 to 35 minutes. Brush biscuits with cold buttermilk.

5. Bake until golden brown, 20 to 25 minutes. Let cool for 10 minutes. Serve with butter.

Fluffy Buttermilk Pancakes

MAKES ABOUT 12 (5- TO 6-INCH) PANCAKES

Whether for breakfast, brunch, breakfast for dinner, or any time in between, the options for serving these flapjacks are endless.

4 cups all-purpose flour
⅓ cup sugar
2 tablespoons baking powder
1 teaspoon kosher salt
4 large eggs
2½ cups whole buttermilk
½ cup unsalted butter, melted and cooled
1 teaspoon vanilla extract
Butter and maple syrup, to serve

1. Preheat oven to 200°. Place a wire rack on a rimmed baking sheet.

2. In a large bowl, whisk together flour, sugar, baking powder, and salt. In another large bowl, whisk together eggs, buttermilk, melted butter, and vanilla. Make a well in center of flour mixture; stir in egg mixture just until combined. (Do not stir until smooth.) Let batter stand.

3. Heat a 10- to 12-inch cast-iron skillet or griddle pan over medium heat. Spray pan with butter-flavored cooking spray.

4. Working in batches, scoop batter by ½ cupfuls onto pan. Cook until edges are dry, bottom is golden brown, and bubbles form on top of pancakes, about 3 minutes. Turn and cook until browned on the bottom, 2 to 3 minutes more. Transfer cooked pancakes to prepared rack, and keep warm in oven until ready to serve.

5. Wipe skillet clean; repeat with cooking spray and remaining batter. Serve with butter and maple syrup.

Sweet Southern Cornbread

MAKES 1 (10-INCH) LOAF

If you prefer your cornbread with a definite sweet side, this version is for you. The mix of equal parts cornmeal and all-purpose flour creates a wonderful not-too-crumbly texture with plenty of corn flavor and those must-have crisp edges.

1¼ cups plain yellow cornmeal
1¼ cups all-purpose flour
2 teaspoons baking powder
1 teaspoon kosher salt
¼ teaspoon baking soda
1¼ cups whole buttermilk
2 large eggs
½ cup firmly packed dark brown sugar
¼ cup unsalted butter, melted and slightly cooled
Butter and honey, to serve

1. Preheat oven to 400°. Spray a 10-inch cast-iron skillet with cooking spray.

2. In a large bowl, whisk together cornmeal, flour, baking powder, salt, and baking soda. In a medium bowl, whisk together buttermilk, eggs, and brown sugar. Stir buttermilk mixture into flour mixture just until combined. Fold in melted butter just until combined. Spread batter into prepared pan.

3. Bake until golden brown and a wooden pick inserted in center comes out clean, 20 to 22 minutes. Let cool in pan for 10 minutes. Serve warm with butter and honey.

Farm Stand Corn Muffins

MAKES 12

When farmers' markets fill with summer produce, this cornbread should move to the top of the list of your must-bake supper sides.

- 1 tablespoon unsalted butter, melted
- 1 cup plain yellow cornmeal
- ¾ cup self-rising flour
- 2½ teaspoons kosher salt, divided
- ½ teaspoon ground black pepper
- 1 cup whole buttermilk
- ¼ cup vegetable oil
- 1 large egg
- ½ cup fresh corn kernels, divided
- 4 tablespoons diced seeded red bell pepper, divided
- 3 tablespoons diced seeded jalapeño, divided
- ¼ cup sliced cherry tomatoes
- 2 tablespoons diced red onion
- 2 tablespoons finely shredded Cheddar cheese
- 2 teaspoons chopped fresh thyme
- ½ cup unsalted butter, softened
- ¼ cup chopped fresh cilantro

1. Preheat oven to 425°. Brush wells of 2 (6-well) cast-iron muffin pans with melted butter. Place pans in oven to preheat for 10 minutes.

2. In a large bowl, whisk together cornmeal, flour, 2 teaspoons salt, and black pepper. In a small bowl, whisk together buttermilk, oil, and egg. Make a well in center of cornmeal mixture; stir in buttermilk mixture, ¼ cup corn kernels, 2 tablespoons bell pepper, and 1½ tablespoons jalapeño just until combined.

3. Carefully remove hot pans from oven. Divide batter among prepared wells. (Batter should sizzle.) Sprinkle with tomatoes, onion, cheese, thyme, remaining ¼ cup corn kernels, remaining 2 tablespoons bell pepper, and remaining 1½ tablespoons jalapeño.

4. Bake until golden brown and a wooden pick inserted in center comes out clean, about 18 minutes. Let cool in pan for 10 minutes.

5. Meanwhile, in a small bowl, stir together softened butter, cilantro, and remaining ½ teaspoon salt until combined. Serve with warm cornbread. Cover and refrigerate remaining cilantro butter for up to 1 week.

Classic Hoecakes

MAKES 28

A cousin to cornbread, hoecakes (also called johnnycakes) pair equally well with sweet and savory toppings. If you don't have bacon drippings on hand, you can use vegetable oil instead.

1 cup all-purpose flour
1 cup plain yellow cornmeal
1 tablespoon sugar
2 teaspoons baking powder
1 teaspoon kosher salt
2 large eggs
¾ cup whole buttermilk
½ cup water
¼ cup vegetable oil
¼ cup bacon drippings
Butter, honey, and pimiento cheese, to serve

1. In a large bowl, whisk together flour, cornmeal, sugar, baking powder, and salt. In a medium bowl, whisk together eggs, buttermilk, ½ cup water, and oil until smooth. Make a well in center of flour mixture; add egg mixture, stirring just until combined. (Batter will be thick.)

2. In a large cast-iron skillet, heat bacon drippings over medium heat. Working in batches, drop 2 tablespoonsful batter into skillet. Cook, turning once, until golden brown, about 2 minutes per side. Serve warm with desired toppings.

Savor the Flavor

An unexpected seasoning or a fresh twist on flavor combinations can take an everyday dish to the next level. This chapter shares some of those delicious upgrades.

BUTTER PAT

Everything Buttermilk Biscuits

MAKES 12

Forget everything bagels—add a schmear of cream cheese or butter to these yummy biscuits instead.

- ½ cup cold salted butter, cubed
- 2½ cups plus 1 tablespoon self-rising flour
- 1 cup cold whole buttermilk
- 1 large egg
- 1 teaspoon water
- 2 tablespoons everything bagel seasoning
- Cream cheese, to serve

1. Lightly spray a 10-inch cast-iron skillet with cooking spray. Line a large rimmed baking sheet with parchment paper.
2. In a large bowl, cut butter into flour using a pastry blender or 2 forks until mixture is crumbly; stir in buttermilk with a fork just until combined.
3. Turn out dough onto a heavily floured surface, and knead several times until dough comes together. Pat or roll dough to ¾-inch thickness. Using a 2¼-inch round cutter dipped in flour, cut dough, without twisting cutter; place biscuits on prepared baking sheet. Reroll scraps and cut as necessary. Freeze biscuits for at least 15 minutes.
4. Preheat oven to 425°.
5. Place biscuits in prepared skillet. In a small bowl, whisk together egg and 1 teaspoon water; brush onto biscuits. Sprinkle with seasoning.
6. Bake until golden brown, 20 to 25 minutes. Let cool in pan on a wire rack for 5 to 10 minutes. Serve warm with cream cheese.

Black Pepper and Thyme Biscuits

MAKES 15

Do you have to make biscuits in a cast-iron skillet? The short answer is no. But try it—the bottoms get extra crispy, kind of like a cracker, and if you pack them in, the sides of the skillet help out with rising.

2 cups all-purpose flour
¼ cup roughly chopped fresh thyme
4 teaspoons baking powder
1 teaspoon kosher salt
¾ teaspoon ground black pepper, divided
¼ teaspoon baking soda
¼ teaspoon garlic powder
¼ teaspoon onion powder
½ cup cold unsalted butter, cubed
1¼ cups whole buttermilk

1. Preheat oven to 450°. Lightly spray a square cast-iron skillet with cooking spray.

2. In a large bowl, whisk together flour, thyme, baking powder, salt, ½ teaspoon pepper, baking soda, garlic powder, and onion powder. Using a pastry blender or 2 forks, cut butter into flour mixture until crumbly. Make a well in flour mixture; add buttermilk, stirring until mixture just comes together.

3. Turn out dough onto a lightly floured surface, and gently pat ¾ inch thick. Using a 2½-inch round cutter dipped in flour, cut 15 biscuits, without twisting cutter, rerolling scraps as necessary. Arrange biscuits in prepared skillet. Sprinkle with remaining ¼ teaspoon pepper.

4. Bake until golden brown, 18 to 20 minutes.

Toad in a Biscuit

MAKES 8

If you've ever had "toad in a hole"—a British dish consisting of an egg fried inside a piece of toast—you should try this version. Using jumbo (the size of a cat's head) biscuits is a fun way to put a Southern twist on the British classic.

2 cups all-purpose flour
1 tablespoon baking powder
1 teaspoon kosher salt
½ teaspoon baking soda
¼ cup cold unsalted butter, cubed
1¼ cups whole buttermilk
½ cup unsalted butter, divided
8 large eggs, separated and divided
Kosher salt
Ground black pepper

1. Preheat oven to 425°.
2. In a large bowl, whisk together flour, baking powder, salt, and baking soda. Using a pastry blender or 2 forks, cut cold butter into flour mixture until crumbly. Make a well in flour mixture; add buttermilk, stirring until mixture just comes together.
3. Using a ½ cup measure, drop dough 2 inches apart on an ungreased baking sheet.
4. Bake until golden brown, about 15 minutes.
5. Using a 2-inch round cutter, cut a hole in center of each biscuit. Reserve cutouts for another use.
6. In a large nonstick skillet, melt ¼ cup butter over medium heat. Place 4 biscuits in skillet, top side down; cook for 1 to 2 minutes. Turn biscuits over. Pour 4 egg whites into holes in biscuits. Cook, without touching, for about 1 minute. Add 4 yolks to whites. Cover and cook to desired degree of doneness, 6 to 7 minutes. Season to taste with salt and pepper. Repeat procedure with remaining butter, biscuits, and eggs. Serve immediately.

Coffee Biscuits and Redeye Gravy

MAKES 8

This recipe adds a surprising ingredient to a traditional biscuit: instant coffee. Topped off with a classic coffee and country ham gravy, it's sure to wake you up!

- 3 cups self-rising flour
- 2 tablespoons plus 1 teaspoon sugar, divided
- 2 tablespoons dark roast instant coffee
- ½ cup cold salted butter, cubed
- ¾ cup plus 2 tablespoons cold whole buttermilk, divided
- 1 large egg
- 1 teaspoon water
- 3 tablespoons unsalted butter, divided
- 1 (6-ounce) package sliced country ham
- 1 cup strong-brewed black coffee
- 1 cup less-sodium chicken broth
- 2 teaspoons smoked paprika
- 1 tablespoon chopped fresh thyme

1. Preheat oven to 425°. Line a baking sheet with parchment paper.

2. In a large bowl, whisk together flour, 2 tablespoons sugar, and instant coffee. Using a pastry blender or 2 forks, cut in cold salted butter until mixture is crumbly. Stir in ¾ cup cold buttermilk with a fork just until combined. Add remaining 2 tablespoons cold buttermilk, if necessary.

3. Turn out dough onto a heavily floured surface, and knead several times until dough holds together. Pat dough to ¾-inch thickness. Using a 2½-inch round cutter, cut dough, rerolling scraps as necessary. Place 2 inches apart on prepared pan. Freeze for 15 minutes.

4. Line a 14-inch round cast-iron baking sheet with parchment paper. Place cold biscuits on pan. In a small bowl, whisk together egg and 1 teaspoon water; brush onto biscuits.

5. Bake until golden brown, 12 to 14 minutes. Serve warm.

6. In a 12-inch cast-iron skillet, melt 1 tablespoon unsalted butter over medium-high heat. Add ham; cook, turning once, until browned, 2 to 3 minutes per side. Remove from skillet, and let drain on paper towels. Reserve drippings in pan.

7. Add brewed coffee to pan, scraping browned bits from bottom of skillet with a wooden spoon. Stir in broth, paprika, and remaining 1 teaspoon sugar; cook, stirring occasionally, until thickened, about 4 minutes. Stir in remaining 2 tablespoons unsalted butter until melted; cook for 1 minute. Remove from heat. Stir in thyme. Serve with ham and coffee biscuits.

Sunday Chicken and Biscuit Pot Pie

MAKES 6 SERVINGS

Some Sundays call for big productions like fried chicken or pot roast. Other times, you're craving a homemade meal that's on the simpler side. This one-skillet wonder fits the bill, packed with plenty of chicken and vegetables and topped with flaky biscuits.

BISCUIT TOPPING

- 1⅓ cups self-rising flour
- 6 tablespoons cold unsalted butter
- ½ cup whole milk

FILLING

- ¼ cup unsalted butter
- 1 cup chopped onion
- 1 cup thinly sliced carrot
- ½ cup chopped celery
- ¼ cup all-purpose flour
- 1 cup chicken broth
- 1 cup half-and-half
- 3 cups chopped cooked chicken
- 1 (9-ounce) package frozen sugar snap peas, thawed
- ½ teaspoon dried thyme
- ½ teaspoon ground black pepper

For the Topping:

1. Preheat oven to 450°. Line a baking sheet with parchment paper. In a large bowl, place flour. Using a pastry blender or 2 forks, cut butter into flour mixture until crumbly. Make a well in flour mixture; add milk, stirring until mixture just comes together.

2. Turn out dough onto a lightly floured surface, and pat dough to ½-inch thickness. Cut dough into rounds with a biscuit cutter or into squares with a knife or pizza cutter. Place biscuits on prepared pan. Parbake for 6 to 8 minutes.

For the Filling:

1. In a 10-inch cast-iron skillet, melt butter over medium heat. Add onion, carrot, and celery; cook until tender, about 8 minutes. Gradually add flour, stirring until combined. Cook for 1 minute, stirring constantly. Gradually add broth and half-and-half; cook, stirring constantly, until mixture thickens, about 5 minutes.

2. Add chicken, peas, thyme, and pepper, stirring to combine. Cook, stirring occasionally, until heated through, about 3 minutes. Place partially baked biscuits on top of chicken mixture. Bake until biscuits are golden brown, 12 to 15 minutes.

Buttermilk Biscuits and Sausage Gravy Cobbler

MAKES 8 SERVINGS

Make your mornings easy with this one-skillet meal combining two Southern favorites. The biscuits can be made ahead of time, so all you have to do is pop them on top of the gravy before transferring the skillet to the oven to bake.

- ½ cup cold salted butter, cubed
- 2½ cups self-rising flour*
- 1 cup cold whole buttermilk
- 1 teaspoon vegetable oil
- 1 (1-pound) package mild breakfast sausage
- 3 tablespoons all-purpose flour
- 2½ cups whole milk
- 1 tablespoon chopped fresh thyme
- 1 teaspoon kosher salt
- 1 teaspoon ground black pepper
- 1 large egg, lightly beaten
- 1 teaspoon water

Garnish: chopped fresh thyme

1. Line a baking sheet with parchment paper.
2. In a large bowl, cut cold butter into flour using a pastry blender or 2 forks until mixture is crumbly. Stir in cold buttermilk with a fork just until combined.
3. Turn out dough onto a heavily floured surface, and knead several times until dough comes together. Pat or roll dough to ¾-inch thickness.
4. Using a 2-inch round cutter dipped in flour, cut dough, without twisting cutter; reroll scraps as necessary. Place 2 inches apart on prepared pan. Freeze for at least 15 minutes or while making gravy.
5. Preheat oven to 425°.
6. In a 12-inch cast-iron skillet, heat oil over medium-high heat. Add sausage; cook until browned and crumbly, about 6 minutes. Stir in flour; cook, stirring constantly, for 1 minute. Gradually whisk in milk, thyme, salt, and pepper until smooth. Remove from heat. Place Buttermilk Biscuits on top of gravy.
7. In a small bowl, whisk together egg and 1 teaspoon water; brush onto biscuits.
8. Bake until biscuits are golden brown and gravy is bubbly, 20 to 22 minutes. Let stand for 5 minutes. Garnish with thyme, if desired.

**We used White Lily Unbleached Self-Rising Flour.*

Savory Cobbler with Sausage and White Beans

MAKES 6 SERVINGS

You'll love what's waiting for you underneath these buttery, crumbly cornbread biscuits—a simmering skillet full of smoked sausage, tender vegetables, and creamy white beans. It's a comfort food masterpiece.

FILLING

- 4 cups sliced smoked sausage
- 1 medium onion, halved and thinly sliced
- 1 green bell pepper, thinly sliced
- 1 red bell pepper, thinly sliced
- 1 tablespoon minced fresh garlic
- 1 teaspoon dried oregano
- ¼ teaspoon crushed red pepper
- 1 (14.5-ounce) can diced tomatoes
- 1 (16-ounce) can white beans, drained and rinsed
- ½ cup water
- 1 teaspoon kosher salt
- ¼ teaspoon ground black pepper

BISCUIT TOPPING

- 1 cup stone-ground white or yellow cornmeal
- 1 cup all-purpose flour
- 2 teaspoons baking powder
- 1 teaspoon kosher salt
- ½ teaspoon baking soda
- 1½ cups whole buttermilk
- ¼ cup unsalted butter, melted
- 1 large egg
- 1 cup grated Parmesan cheese

For the Filling:

1. In a 12-inch cast-iron skillet, cook sausage over medium-high heat until browned, about 4 minutes. Remove sausage using a slotted spoon, and let drain on paper towels.

2. Add onion, bell peppers, garlic, oregano, and red pepper to skillet. Cook, stirring occasionally, until vegetables are tender, about 5 minutes. Add tomatoes to skillet; cook for 2 minutes. Stir in sausage, beans, ½ cup water, salt, and black pepper; bring to a boil. Remove from heat.

For the Topping:

1. Preheat oven to 425°. In a medium bowl, stir together cornmeal, flour, baking powder, salt, and baking soda. In another medium bowl, stir together buttermilk, melted butter, and egg. Gradually add buttermilk mixture to cornmeal mixture, stirring just until combined. Stir in cheese. Drop batter by heaping tablespoonfuls over sausage filling.

2. Bake until topping is golden brown, 15 to 18 minutes.

Biscuit-Topped Chicken Pot Pies

MAKES 8

Their easy preparation makes drop biscuits a perfect topping for pot pies, like these little guys. A sprinkle of sharp white Cheddar cheese makes them even better.

- **2 tablespoons vegetable oil**
- **2 cups chopped yellow onion**
- **⅔ cup chopped carrot**
- **⅓ cup finely chopped celery**
- **2½ cups all-purpose flour, divided**
- **3 cups less-sodium chicken broth**
- **½ cup heavy whipping cream**
- **½ cup whole milk**
- **4 cups shredded cooked chicken**
- **4 cups chopped fresh kale**
- **2 teaspoons kosher salt, divided**
- **1 teaspoon ground black pepper**
- **1½ cups finely shredded sharp white Cheddar cheese, divided**
- **1½ teaspoons baking powder**
- **½ teaspoon baking soda**
- **5 tablespoons cold unsalted butter, cubed**
- **1 cup whole buttermilk**

1. Preheat oven to 400°. Line a baking sheet with parchment paper.

2. In a large Dutch oven, heat oil over medium-high heat. Add onion, carrot, and celery; cook, stirring frequently, until vegetables soften, about 5 minutes. Add ½ cup flour; cook for 1 minute. Add broth, and bring to a boil, stirring until mixture thickens, about 1 minute. Reduce heat to medium-low; stir in cream and milk. Add chicken and kale; cook for 8 minutes, stirring frequently. Add 1 teaspoon salt and pepper, stirring to combine. Divide mixture among 8 (1-cup) ovenproof ramekins.

3. In a large bowl, whisk together 1 cup cheese, baking powder, baking soda, remaining 2 cups flour, and remaining 1 teaspoon salt. Using a pastry blender or 2 forks, cut butter into flour mixture until crumbly. Make a well in flour mixture; add buttermilk, stirring until mixture just comes together. (Dough will be sticky.) Drop heaping ¼ cupfuls of dough onto prepared pan.

4. Bake until edges are lightly browned, about 8 minutes. Place ramekins on a rimmed baking sheet. Place biscuits on top of ramekins, and sprinkle with remaining ½ cup cheese. Bake until browned and bubbly, 12 to 16 minutes, covering with foil to prevent excess browning, if necessary.

Chicken and Dumplings Skillet Casserole

MAKES 4 SERVINGS

For many, chicken and dumplings is a nostalgic dish and one of the most adored comfort foods. This casserole version trades pillowy simmered dumplings for a quick biscuit topping that bakes up nice and flaky.

FILLING

- 4 boneless skinless chicken thighs, halved
- 1 teaspoon kosher salt, divided
- ½ teaspoon ground black pepper, divided
- 5 teaspoons vegetable oil, divided
- 1½ cups fresh green beans, chopped
- 1 cup chopped parsnip
- 1 cup quartered mushrooms
- ½ cup chopped carrot
- 1¼ cups chicken broth
- ¼ cup all-purpose flour
- ½ cup whole milk
- 1 tablespoon chopped fresh parsley
- 1 teaspoon chopped fresh rosemary

BISCUIT TOPPING

- 1 cup self-rising flour
- ¼ cup cold unsalted butter, cubed
- ¼ cup whole milk
- 1 tablespoon butter, melted

For the Filling:

1. Sprinkle chicken with ¼ teaspoon salt and ¼ teaspoon pepper. In a 10-inch ovenproof skillet, heat 2 teaspoons oil over medium-high heat. Add chicken; cook until browned, about 2 minutes per side. Remove from pan; set aside.

2. Wipe skillet clean. Heat remaining 3 teaspoons oil in skillet over medium-high heat. Add green beans, parsnip, mushrooms, and carrot; cook, stirring occasionally, until vegetables begin to soften, about 4 minutes. Add broth. Reduce heat to medium-low; cover and simmer until tender, about 10 minutes. In a medium bowl, stir together flour, remaining ¾ teaspoon salt, and remaining ¼ teaspoon pepper. Whisk in milk, parsley, and rosemary. Add to vegetable mixture in pan, stirring until mixture begins to thicken. Return chicken to pan. Cover and remove from heat.

For the Topping:

1. Preheat oven to 400°. In the work bowl of a food processor, pulse flour and butter until mixture is crumbly. Add milk, 1 tablespoon at a time, pulsing until a soft dough forms. Turn out dough onto a lightly floured surface, and knead 3 or 4 times. Roll dough to ½-inch thickness, and cut into 1-inch pieces.

2. Place dough pieces on top of hot filling in skillet. Bake until biscuits are lightly browned and chicken is cooked through, about 15 minutes. Brush tops of biscuits with melted butter before serving.

Garlic-Caraway Soda Bread

MAKES 1 (9-INCH) LOAF

This adaptation of the classic Irish bread features citrusy-peppery caraway seeds, which give rye bread its signature flavor.

3⅔ cups all-purpose flour
2 teaspoons minced garlic
2 teaspoons kosher salt
1½ teaspoons caraway seeds
½ teaspoon baking soda
¼ teaspoon ground black pepper
2 cups whole buttermilk
Butter, to serve

1. Preheat oven to 450°. Line an 8-inch cast-iron skillet with parchment paper, letting excess extend over sides of pan.

2. In a large bowl, whisk together flour, garlic, salt, caraway seeds, baking soda, and pepper until well combined; make a well in center. Using your hand, stir in buttermilk just until combined and a dough begins to form. (Dough should be sticky and slightly clumpy.)

3. Turn out dough onto a lightly floured surface. Using floured hands, gently shape dough into a round. Turn dough over, and gently shape dough into an even round. Transfer dough to prepared skillet, and gently flatten to fill skillet.

4. Using a knife dipped in flour, cut a 1-inch-deep X across top of dough. Using tip of knife, prick a hole into each section of dough.

5. Bake for 15 minutes. Reduce oven temperature to 400°. Bake until golden brown and an instant-read thermometer inserted in center registers 200°, 10 to 15 minutes more. Let cool in pan on a wire rack for 10 minutes. Serve warm with butter.

Chive and Dill Popovers

MAKES 18

These golden, herb-infused breads are crisp and flaky on the outside with a buttery interior. You can substitute any combination of fresh herbs that you like.

- 2 cups bread flour
- 1¼ teaspoons kosher salt
- 1 teaspoon sugar
- ½ teaspoon ground black pepper
- 2 cups whole milk, room temperature
- 3 large eggs, room temperature
- 3 tablespoons unsalted butter, melted
- 1 tablespoon minced fresh chives
- 1 tablespoon minced fresh dill
- Shortening, for greasing pans

1. In a medium bowl, whisk together flour, salt, sugar, and pepper. In a large glass measuring cup, whisk together milk, eggs, melted butter, chives, and dill until combined. Whisk flour mixture into milk mixture until smooth and well combined. Cover and let stand at room temperature for 1 hour.

2. Preheat oven to 400°. Grease bottom and sides of 3 (6-cup) cast-iron muffin pans with shortening. Place pans on a large baking sheet.

3. Whisk batter; pour into prepared pans, filling cups almost full.

4. Bake until golden brown and puffed, 30 to 35 minutes. Serve hot.

Peppery Flatbreads

MAKES 8

Whip up these breads in less than 30 minutes using pantry staples you probably already have on hand. You can serve flatbreads as a side or use them as a base for mini pizzas and wraps or pair them with hummus and other dips.

2¾ cups self-rising flour
½ teaspoon kosher salt
½ teaspoon coarsely ground black pepper
2 cups plain whole Greek yogurt
Canola oil, for greasing pan

1. In a large bowl, stir together flour, salt, pepper, and yogurt just until yogurt is mostly combined. Knead until a dough forms. (Dough will be sticky.) Divide dough into 8 portions.

2. Place one portion of dough on a heavily floured surface; heavily flour top of dough, and roll to an 8-inch round. Repeat with remaining dough.

3. Heat a cast-iron griddle over medium heat until hot. Spread about 1 teaspoon oil onto pan. Place one dough round on hot griddle. Cook until puffed and golden brown in spots on bottom, about 2 minutes. Turn and cook 2 minutes more. Wipe excess flour off griddle. Repeat with oil, as needed, and remaining dough. Serve warm.

Bacon Upside-Down Cornbread

MAKES 1 (10-INCH) LOAF

Loaded with Gruyère cheese, fresh herbs, and bacon, this hearty cornbread is practically a meal in itself!

11 slices thick-cut bacon, divided
Melted bacon drippings or vegetable oil, as needed
2 cups white cornmeal
1 cup all-purpose flour
1 tablespoon baking powder
1 tablespoon chopped fresh thyme
1½ teaspoons kosher salt
½ teaspoon ground black pepper
2½ cups whole buttermilk
2 large eggs
1½ cups shredded Gruyère cheese
Garnish: chopped fresh thyme

1. Preheat oven to 425°.

2. In a 10-inch cast-iron skillet, cook 5 slices bacon over medium-high heat until almost crisp, about 10 minutes. Remove bacon, and let drain on paper towels. Chop remaining 6 slices bacon. Add chopped bacon to pan; cook, stirring occasionally, until crisp, about 12 minutes. Remove chopped bacon using a slotted spoon, and let drain on paper towels. Pour off drippings into a small bowl, adding more melted bacon drippings or oil as needed to equal 8 tablespoons. Wipe skillet clean.

3. Add 2 tablespoons reserved bacon drippings to skillet, and place in oven to preheat, about 8 minutes.

4. In a large bowl, whisk together cornmeal, flour, baking powder, thyme, salt, and pepper. In a small bowl, whisk together buttermilk, eggs, and remaining 6 tablespoons reserved bacon drippings. Make a well in center of cornmeal mixture. Add buttermilk mixture, stirring until just combined. Stir in cheese and reserved chopped bacon until just combined. Carefully place reserved 5 slices bacon in bottom of preheated skillet. Pour batter onto slices.

5. Bake until golden brown and a wooden pick inserted in center comes out clean, about 30 minutes. Let cool in pan on a wire rack for 10 minutes. Invert onto a serving plate. Garnish with thyme, if desired.

Cornbread Scones

MAKES 8

An across-the-pond snack meets Southern goodness in these crispy, fluffy wedges that are best served with generous slathers of butter.

- **1 cup plain yellow cornmeal**
- **1 cup all-purpose flour**
- **2 tablespoons sugar**
- **2½ teaspoons baking powder**
- **1¼ teaspoons kosher salt, divided**
- **⅓ cup cold unsalted butter, cubed**
- **½ cup whole buttermilk**
- **2 large eggs, divided**
- **Butter, to serve**

1. Line a small baking sheet with parchment paper.
2. In a large bowl, whisk together cornmeal, flour, sugar, baking powder, and 1 teaspoon salt. Using a pastry blender or 2 forks, cut butter into flour mixture until it resembles coarse crumbs.
3. In a small bowl, whisk together buttermilk and 1 egg. Stir buttermilk mixture into flour mixture with a fork until a dough begins to form.
4. Turn out dough onto a heavily floured surface, and gently fold and pat dough until smooth, 4 to 5 times. Gently press dough into a 6-inch circle. Cut into 8 wedges. Place wedges on prepared baking sheet, and refrigerate for 10 minutes.
5. Preheat oven to 375°. Spray wells of an 8-well cast-iron wedge pan with cooking spray.
6. In a small bowl, whisk together remaining egg and remaining ¼ teaspoon salt. Place dough wedges in pan; brush with egg mixture. Bake until lightly browned and a wooden pick inserted in center comes out clean, about 15 minutes. Let cool in pan for 5 minutes. Serve warm with butter.

Bacon-Blueberry Hoecakes with Bacon Butter

MAKES ABOUT 14

With a little bit of sweet and savory in every bite, these chewy-on-the-inside, crispy-on-the-outside Southern-style cakes are griddled to perfection.

- 10 slices thick-cut bacon, finely chopped
- ¼ cup salted butter, softened
- 1 cup self-rising flour
- 1 cup self-rising yellow cornmeal mix
- ¾ cup whole buttermilk
- ⅓ cup water
- 2 large eggs, lightly beaten
- 2 tablespoons maple syrup, plus more for serving
- 1 teaspoon vanilla extract
- 1 cup fresh blueberries, plus more for serving

1. In a 12-inch cast-iron skillet, cook bacon over medium-low heat, stirring occasionally, until crisp, 4 to 5 minutes. Using a slotted spoon, remove bacon, and let drain on paper towels. Pour off drippings into a small bowl; reserve.

2. In a small bowl, stir together ¼ cup cooked chopped bacon and softened butter; reserve.

3. In a large bowl, whisk together flour, cornmeal mix, and remaining chopped bacon. In a medium bowl, whisk together buttermilk, ⅓ cup water, eggs, 2 tablespoons maple syrup, and vanilla. Make a well in center of flour mixture; stir in buttermilk mixture until well combined. Gently fold in 1 cup blueberries.

4. In same skillet, heat 3 tablespoons reserved bacon drippings over medium heat. Drop batter by 2 tablespoonfuls into hot drippings; cook until bottom is browned and crisp, 2 to 3 minutes. Turn and cook until bottom is browned, about 2 minutes more. Let hoecakes drain briefly on paper towels. Repeat with remaining drippings and remaining batter. Serve with bacon butter, maple syrup, and blueberries.

Cheesy Comforts

If you are in search of savory comfort food, you are in the right place. There's cheesy goodness of all varieties found in every bite.

Herb and Cheese Drop Biscuits

MAKES 12

These savory biscuits are easy to make. The mayonnaise adds richness and moisture to the biscuits. They're so good; you'll want to add them to your weekly rotation.

BISCUITS

4 cups all-purpose flour
2 teaspoons baking powder
1 teaspoon baking soda
2½ teaspoons kosher salt
¼ teaspoon ground black pepper
Lemon-Garlic Mayo (recipe follows)
2½ cups cold whole buttermilk
1 (4-ounce) wedge Parmesan cheese, freshly grated
½ cup chopped fresh basil

LEMON-GARLIC MAYO
Makes about ½ cup

½ cup mayonnaise
1 teaspoon Dijon mustard
2 cloves garlic, grated
½ teaspoon lemon zest

For the Biscuits:

1. Preheat oven to 375°. Spray the griddle side of a reversible 19-inch rectangular cast-iron grill/griddle pan with cooking spray.

2. In a large bowl, whisk together flour, baking powder, baking soda, salt, and pepper. Whisk in Lemon-Garlic Mayo and buttermilk just until combined. Fold in Parmesan and basil. Drop batter by ⅓ cupfuls onto prepared pan.

3. Bake until golden brown, 15 to 18 minutes. Let cool in pan for 5 minutes. Serve warm.

For the Mayo:

1. In a small bowl, whisk together all ingredients. Cover and refrigerate until using.

Bacon-Cheddar Biscuits

MAKES 14

Add bacon fat to a classic biscuit recipe? There's only one thing to say—yes! Bacon makes everything better, right?

- **2½ cups self-rising flour**
- **1 tablespoon sugar**
- **1 teaspoon ground black pepper**
- **½ cup cold bacon drippings**
- **2 tablespoons cold unsalted butter, cubed**
- **1 cup shredded sharp Cheddar cheese**
- **½ cup crumbled cooked bacon**
- **¾ cup cold whole buttermilk**
- **2 tablespoons unsalted butter, melted**

1. Preheat oven to 425°. Line a baking sheet with parchment paper.

2. In a large bowl, stir together flour, sugar, and pepper. Using a pastry blender or 2 forks, cut in bacon drippings and cold butter until crumbly. Stir in cheese, cooked bacon, and buttermilk just until combined.

3. Turn out dough onto a heavily floured surface. Fold dough in half until it just comes together, 3 to 4 times. Pat or roll dough into a 1-inch-thick rectangle. Using a knife dipped in flour, cut dough into 2-inch rectangles.

4. Place biscuits 2 inches apart on prepared pan. Freeze until cold, about 10 minutes. Brush with melted butter. Bake until golden brown, about 12 minutes.

Spicy Cheddar Biscuits with Glazed Ham

MAKES 10

For lunch, for brunch, or even for parties, it's hard to pass up a good ham biscuit. This sweet and smoky ham is especially delicious on these cheesy biscuits.

SPICY CHEDDAR BICUITS

- 2 cups all-purpose flour
- 1 tablespoon baking powder
- ½ teaspoon kosher salt
- ½ teaspoon ground red pepper
- ½ cup cold unsalted butter, cubed
- ⅔ cup shredded sharp Cheddar cheese
- 1 cup whole buttermilk
- Melted butter
- Sliced Glazed Ham (recipe follows) and honey, to serve

GLAZED HAM

Makes 10 to 12 servings

- 1¼ cups water, divided
- 1 (10- to 11-pound) bone-in smoked ham (shank portion)
- ⅔ cup firmly packed light brown sugar
- ⅔ cup cane syrup
- ⅓ cup distilled white vinegar
- 2 teaspoons smoked paprika
- ¼ teaspoon kosher salt

For the Biscuits:

1. Preheat oven to 425°. Line a large baking sheet with parchment paper.

2. In the work bowl of a food processor, place flour, baking powder, salt, and red pepper; pulse until combined. Add butter; pulse until crumbly, 4 to 5 times. Add cheese and ¾ cup buttermilk; pulse just until dry ingredients are moistened. Gradually add remaining ¼ cup buttermilk, if needed.

3. Turn out dough onto a lightly floured surface, and gently knead 3 times. Roll dough ½ inch thick. Fold dough in half. Using a 2½-inch round cutter dipped in flour, cut 10 biscuits, without twisting cutter, rerolling scraps once. Place biscuits 1 inch apart on prepared pan. Bake until lightly browned, about 12 minutes. Brush with melted butter. Cut biscuits in half. Serve with Glazed Ham and honey.

For the Ham:

1. Preheat oven to 325°. Line a roasting pan with foil, and spray with cooking spray. Pour 1 cup water in pan. Using a sharp knife, lightly score outside of ham. Place ham in prepared pan, and loosely cover with foil. Bake for 1 hour.

2. In a bowl, whisk together brown sugar, cane syrup, vinegar, paprika, salt, and remaining ¼ cup water. Brush ham with sugar mixture. Bake, loosely covered with foil, until a meat thermometer registers 160°, about 1 hour and 30 minutes more, brushing with sugar mixture occasionally. (Add additional water to pan, if needed.)

Cheesy Pepper Biscuits

MAKES 25

Round biscuits are often the default, so serving square ones can be a fun change. Another perk: These biscuits don't require a special cutter—any good knife will do the trick.

2 cups all-purpose flour
1 tablespoon baking powder
¾ teaspoon kosher salt
½ teaspoon sugar
¼ teaspoon cracked black pepper
¼ teaspoon ground red pepper
½ cup cold unsalted butter, cubed
⅔ cup shredded sharp Cheddar cheese
¼ cup freshly grated Parmesan cheese
1 cup whole buttermilk
1 tablespoon unsalted butter, melted
Stone-ground mustard and ham, to serve

1. Preheat oven to 425°.

2. In a large bowl, whisk together flour, baking powder, salt, sugar, black pepper, and red pepper. Using a pastry blender or 2 forks, cut butter into flour mixture until crumbly. Make a well in flour mixture; add cheeses and ¾ cup buttermilk, stirring until mixture just comes together. Add remaining ¼ cup buttermilk, if needed.

3. On a lightly floured surface, gently knead dough 4 or 5 times. Roll or pat dough into an 8-inch square; cut into 25 squares. Place close together in a 10-inch square cast-iron skillet or a parchment-lined baking sheet.

4. Bake until golden brown, about 17 minutes. Let cool for 15 minutes. Using a large spatula, remove from pan, and separate biscuits. Split biscuits horizontally, and brush with melted butter. Serve with mustard and ham.

Black Pepper and Parmesan Biscuits with Roast Beef

MAKES 10

Roast beef and horseradish are a classic pairing for a reason—the flavor combination is hard to beat. These sandwiches make a great appetizer for any party or gathering.

- 3 cups self-rising flour
- ½ cup cold unsalted butter, cubed
- ½ cup freshly grated Parmesan cheese
- 2 teaspoons coarsely ground black pepper
- 1¼ cups whole buttermilk
- 1 cup mayonnaise
- 2 tablespoons horseradish
- 1 pound thinly sliced deli roast beef

1. Preheat oven to 450°. Line a baking sheet with parchment paper.

2. In a medium bowl, place flour. Using a pastry blender or 2 forks, cut butter into flour until crumbly. Stir in cheese and pepper. Make a well in flour mixture; add buttermilk, stirring until mixture just comes together.

3. On a lightly floured surface, pat dough into a ¾-inch-thick circle. Using a 2½-inch round cutter dipped in flour, cut 10 biscuits, without twisting cutter, discarding scraps. Place biscuits on prepared pan.

4. Bake until lightly browned, 12 to 15 minutes.

5. In a small bowl, combine mayonnaise and horseradish. Cut biscuits in half, and spread cut sides of biscuits with mayonnaise mixture. Top bottom halves with roast beef, and cover with top halves of biscuits.

Hot Cheddar Biscuits with Spicy Honey

MAKES 10

This crave-worthy sweet and savory combination is sure to bring some spice to your life. If you need to tame the heat, you can reduce the hot sauce to your preferred heat level.

- **3½ cups all-purpose flour**
- **2 tablespoons baking powder**
- **1 tablespoon sugar**
- **½ teaspoon ground red pepper**
- **½ teaspoon kosher salt**
- **⅔ cup cold unsalted butter, cubed**
- **2 cups shredded sharp Cheddar cheese**
- **1 cup cold whole buttermilk**
- **¼ cup plus 1 tablespoon hot sauce, divided**
- **½ cup honey**

1. Preheat oven to 450°. Line a cast-iron baking pan with parchment paper.
2. In a large bowl, whisk together flour, baking powder, sugar, red pepper, and salt. Using a pastry blender or 2 forks, cut in cold butter until mixture resembles coarse meal; stir in cheese.
3. In a small bowl, stir together buttermilk and ¼ cup hot sauce; stir into flour mixture until combined. Turn out dough onto a floured work surface. Gently knead dough just until it comes together, about 8 times. Roll out dough to 1-inch thickness. Using a 3-inch round cutter, cut 10 biscuits, without twisting cutter, discarding scraps. Place biscuits on prepared pan.
4. Bake until puffed and lightly browned, 14 to 16 minutes. Let cool for 5 minutes.
5. In a small bowl, stir together honey and remaining 1 tablespoon hot sauce; serve with warm biscuits.

Cheddar Biscuits with Fresh Herbs

MAKES 12

Second to their inherent goodness, one of the best things about biscuits is that you can make them ahead of time, and they freeze beautifully. Do your future self a favor, and make a batch of these herbed beauties to keep in the freezer to have on hand for the next time you need an easy side dish for dinner or when a craving strikes.

- **3 cups all-purpose flour**
- **1 tablespoon baking powder**
- **1 teaspoon kosher salt**
- **½ teaspoon baking soda**
- **½ cup cold unsalted butter, cubed**
- **½ cup shredded sharp Cheddar cheese**
- **1 tablespoon chopped fresh parsley**
- **1 tablespoon chopped fresh chives**
- **1 tablespoon chopped fresh rosemary**
- **1½ cups plus 2 to 4 tablespoons heavy whipping cream, divided**

1. Preheat oven to 450°. Line a baking sheet with parchment paper.

2. In a large bowl, whisk together flour, baking powder, salt, and baking soda. Using a pastry blender or 2 forks, cut butter into flour mixture until crumbly. Fold in cheese, parsley, chives, and rosemary. Make a well in flour mixture; add 1½ cups cream, stirring until mixture just comes together. Add additional 2 tablespoons cream, if necessary.

3. Turn out dough onto a lightly floured surface, and knead lightly 3 to 4 times. Pat dough to ½-inch thickness. Using a 3-inch round cutter dipped in flour, cut 12 biscuits, without twisting cutter, rerolling scraps once.

4. Place biscuits 1 inch apart on prepared pan. Using a pastry brush, lightly brush tops of biscuits with remaining 2 tablespoons cream.

5. Bake until light golden brown, 12 to 15 minutes. Serve warm.

Cornmeal Cheddar Biscuits

MAKES ABOUT 9

Cornmeal adds a slight sweetness and crunch to these biscuits. Use a soft wheat all-purpose flour such as White Lily to keep them fluffy.

- **1⅔ cups all-purpose flour**
- **¼ cup plain yellow cornmeal**
- **1 tablespoon baking powder**
- **1 teaspoon sugar**
- **½ teaspoon kosher salt**
- **6 tablespoons cold unsalted butter, cubed**
- **½ cup finely shredded sharp white Cheddar cheese**
- **1 cup cold whole buttermilk**
- **2 teaspoons vegetable oil**
- **2 tablespoons unsalted butter, melted**

1. Preheat oven to 450°. Line a small baking sheet with parchment paper.

2. In a large bowl, whisk together flour, cornmeal, baking powder, sugar, and salt. Using a pastry blender or 2 forks, cut in cold butter until mixture is crumbly and some pea-size pieces of butter remain. Stir in cheese. Add buttermilk, stirring just until dry ingredients are moistened.

3. On a floured surface, gently knead dough 4 to 6 times. (Dough will be sticky.) Roll dough to ½-inch thickness. Fold dough in half, and roll to ¾-inch thickness. Using a 2½-inch round cutter dipped in flour, cut dough, rerolling scraps once. Place biscuits on prepared pan. Place biscuits in freezer while cast-iron pan preheats.

4. Brush a 14-inch cast-iron baking pan with oil; place pan in oven until very hot, about 5 minutes. Remove biscuits from baking sheet, and place 1 inch apart on preheated pan.

5. Bake until golden brown, about 12 minutes. Brush with melted butter. Serve warm.

Cheese and Herb Angel Biscuits

MAKES ABOUT 13

These cheesy, herb-flecked biscuits are light and fluffy thanks to the addition of three leaveners: yeast, baking powder, and baking soda.

- **¼ cup warm water (105° to 110°)**
- **1 tablespoon sugar**
- **1 (0.25-ounce) package active dry yeast**
- **2½ cups all-purpose flour**
- **1½ teaspoons baking powder**
- **1 teaspoon flaked sea salt**
- **½ teaspoon baking soda**
- **½ cup all-vegetable shortening, room temperature**
- **¾ cup whole buttermilk, room temperature**
- **½ cup shredded sharp Cheddar cheese**
- **½ cup shredded extra-sharp white Cheddar cheese**
- **2 teaspoons chopped fresh chives**
- **2 teaspoons chopped fresh dill**
- **1 teaspoon chopped fresh thyme**
- **2 tablespoons salted butter, melted**

Garnish: melted butter, flaked sea salt, chopped fresh herbs

1. In a small bowl, stir together ¼ cup warm water, sugar, and yeast. Let stand until mixture is foamy, about 5 minutes.

2. In a large bowl, whisk together flour, baking powder, sea salt, and baking soda. Using a pastry blender or 2 forks, cut in shortening until mixture is crumbly. Stir in yeast mixture and buttermilk just until dry ingredients are moistened. Stir in cheeses and herbs just until combined.

3. Spray a 12-inch cast-iron skillet with cooking spray. Turn out dough onto a lightly floured surface, and knead for 1 minute. Roll dough to ½-inch thickness. Using a 2-inch round cutter, cut dough without twisting cutter, and place in prepared skillet. Loosely cover with plastic wrap, and let stand in a warm, draft-free place (75°) until slightly risen, 45 minutes to 1 hour.

4. Preheat oven to 400°.

5. Brush dough with melted butter. Bake until golden brown, 12 to 14 minutes. Garnish with butter, sea salt, and herbs, if desired. Serve warm.

Cheesy Bacon Biscuit Bites

MAKES 32

These biscuit bites are ideal when you need a quick side for dinner or you're in charge of bringing something for a get-together, and they're sure to be a hit. A golden-brown biscuit exterior conceals the center filled with gooey cheese and smoky bacon. It's heaven in a bite.

2 (16.3-ounce) cans refrigerated homestyle biscuits*
1 (8-ounce) package shredded Colby-Jack cheese
1 (12-ounce) package thick-cut bacon, chopped and cooked
1 large egg, lightly beaten
Everything bagel seasoning

1. Preheat oven to 350°. Spray a 12-inch cast-iron skillet with baking spray with flour.

2. On a clean work surface, cut each biscuit in half crosswise. Gently press each biscuit piece to ¼-inch thickness. Add about 1 tablespoon cheese and 1 teaspoon bacon to center of each dough piece; wrap dough around filling, pinching seams to seal. Starting at sides of pan, place biscuits, seam side down, in concentric circles. (Biscuits will fit snuggly, with sides touching, in pan.) Brush egg onto biscuits; sprinkle with everything bagel seasoning.

3. Bake until golden brown, 28 to 30 minutes. Let cool in pan for 10 minutes. Serve warm.

**We used Pillsbury Grands! Southern Homestyle Buttermilk Biscuits.*

Pepper Jack-Bacon Scones

MAKES 8

A cast-iron wedge pan makes these cheesy scones wonderfully crisp on the outside. You can also bake the wedges in a 10-inch cast-iron skillet, in a cast-iron baking pan, or on a traditional baking sheet.

2 cups all-purpose flour
1 tablespoon baking powder
¾ teaspoon kosher salt
¼ teaspoon ground black pepper
¼ teaspoon smoked paprika
6 tablespoons cold unsalted butter, cubed
¾ cup shredded Monterey Jack cheese with peppers, divided
4 slices bacon, cooked and crumbled
1 small jalapeño, seeded and minced
1 cup whole buttermilk
1 large egg

1. Preheat oven to 425°. Spray an 8-well cast-iron wedge pan with cooking spray.

2. In a large bowl, whisk together flour, baking powder, salt, pepper, and paprika. Using a pastry blender or 2 forks, cut in cold butter until mixture is crumbly. Stir in ½ cup cheese, bacon, and jalapeño.

3. In a small bowl, whisk together buttermilk and egg; add buttermilk mixture to flour mixture, stirring just until combined.

4. Turn out dough onto a heavily floured surface, and knead until dough comes together, 4 to 5 times. Pat or roll dough into a 1-inch-thick circle. Cut into 8 wedges. Place wedges in prepared wells. Sprinkle with remaining ¼ cup cheese.

5. Bake until golden brown and a wooden pick inserted in center comes out clean, about 20 minutes. Serve warm.

Parmesan-Herb Buttermilk Bread

MAKES 1 (8X4-INCH) LOAF

Buttermilk and baking powder help this loaf rise almost like a yeasted bread—no proofing required.

- **2½ cups all-purpose flour**
- **3 tablespoons sugar**
- **2½ teaspoons baking powder**
- **¾ teaspoon kosher salt**
- **1 large egg**
- **1⅓ cups whole buttermilk**
- **¼ cup canola oil**
- **⅔ cup plus 2 tablespoons freshly grated Parmesan cheese, divided**
- **⅓ cup chopped assorted fresh herbs (such as parsley, thyme, and basil)**

1. Preheat oven to 350°. Spray an 8x4-inch cast-iron loaf pan with baking spray with flour.

2. In a large bowl, whisk together flour, sugar, baking powder, and salt. In a medium bowl, whisk together egg, buttermilk, and oil. Stir egg mixture into flour mixture until well combined; stir in ⅔ cup cheese and herbs. Spread batter into prepared pan; sprinkle with remaining 2 tablespoons cheese.

3. Bake until a wooden pick inserted in center comes out clean, 50 to 55 minutes. Let cool in pan on a wire rack for 10 minutes. Remove from pan, and let cool completely on a wire rack.

Cheddar and Sage Beer Bread

MAKES 1 (8X4-INCH) LOAF

Rich, malty amber ale adds depth of flavor and helps create a tender crumb in this savory loaf.

3 cups plus 2 tablespoons self-rising flour
2 tablespoons sugar
1 tablespoon chopped fresh sage
1 cup shredded extra-sharp Cheddar cheese
1 (12-ounce) bottle amber ale
2 tablespoons unsalted butter, melted
½ teaspoon kosher salt
Fresh sage leaves (optional)

1. Preheat oven to 375°. Spray an 8x4-inch cast-iron loaf pan with baking spray with flour.

2. In a large bowl, whisk together flour, sugar, and chopped sage; stir in cheese. Stir in beer just until combined. Spread batter into prepared pan. Drizzle melted butter onto batter; sprinkle with salt. Gently press sage leaves onto batter, if desired.

3. Bake until golden brown and a wooden pick inserted in center comes out clean, 45 to 50 minutes. Let cool in pan on a wire rack for 10 minutes. Remove from pan, and let cool on a wire rack for 20 minutes; serve warm.

Smoked Cheddar Corn Muffins

MAKES 12

These muffins are smoky with a savory bite of green onion. They are an ideal companion for soups, stews, and other hearty meals.

- **1 cup self-rising yellow cornmeal**
- **1/3 cup self-rising flour**
- **2 tablespoons sugar**
- **1/2 teaspoon kosher salt**
- **1/4 teaspoon ground red pepper**
- **3/4 cup whole milk**
- **1/4 cup chopped green onion**
- **1/4 cup unsalted butter, melted**
- **2 large eggs, lightly beaten**
- **1 cup shredded smoked Cheddar cheese**

Butter, to serve

1. Preheat oven to 425°. Spray 2 (6-cup) cast-iron muffin pans with cooking spray. Place pans in oven to preheat.

2. In a large bowl, stir together cornmeal, flour, sugar, salt, and red pepper. In a small bowl, whisk together milk, green onion, melted butter, and eggs. Add milk mixture to cornmeal mixture, stirring to combine. Add cheese, stirring just until combined. Carefully remove pans from oven. Divide batter among prepared pans.

3. Bake until golden brown, about 15 minutes. Let cool in pans for 5 minutes. Serve warm with butter.

Bacon-Pimiento Cheese Cornbread

MAKES 1 (10-INCH) LOAF

You could make a meal out of this decadent, crunchy-bottomed cornbread that's loaded with crispy bacon and creamy pimiento cheese.

½ pound bacon, chopped
2 cups plain yellow cornmeal
1 cup all-purpose flour
1 tablespoon baking powder
1½ teaspoons kosher salt
2 large eggs
2½ cups whole buttermilk
4 tablespoons unsalted butter, melted
2 cups pimiento cheese*, divided

1. Preheat oven to 425°.

2. In a 10-inch cast-iron skillet, cook bacon over medium heat until browned and crisp. Remove bacon using a slotted spoon, and let drain on paper towels, reserving 2 tablespoons drippings in skillet.

3. Place skillet with drippings in oven until very hot, about 3 minutes.

4. In a large bowl, whisk together cornmeal, flour, baking powder, and salt. In a medium bowl, whisk together eggs, buttermilk, and melted butter. Stir egg mixture into cornmeal mixture just until dry ingredients are moistened; stir in ½ cup bacon and 1 cup pimiento cheese. Carefully spread batter into hot skillet.

5. Bake until golden brown and a wooden pick inserted in center comes out clean, about 25 minutes.

6. In a small bowl, stir together remaining bacon and remaining 1 cup pimiento cheese. Serve with hot cornbread.

**We used Pawleys Island Palmetto Cheese.*

Spicy Beer Cheese Cornbread

MAKES 1 (10-INCH) LOAF

The use of beer in this cornbread batter adds moisture and makes the finished product deliciously dense.

- 1 tablespoon canola oil
- 2 cups stone-ground fine yellow cornmeal
- 1 cup all-purpose flour
- 2 tablespoons sugar
- 1 tablespoon baking powder
- 1½ teaspoons kosher salt
- 1 (12-ounce) bottle amber beer
- 1¼ cups whole buttermilk
- 6 tablespoons unsalted butter, melted
- 2 large eggs, beaten
- 1½ cups shredded Cheddar cheese
- ⅔ cup candied jalapeño slices, plus more for garnish

1. Preheat oven to 425°. Add oil to a 10-inch cast-iron skillet. Place pan in oven until oil is very hot, about 8 minutes.

2. In a large bowl, whisk together cornmeal, flour, sugar, baking powder, and salt; make a well in center of cornmeal mixture. Stir beer, buttermilk, melted butter, and eggs into cornmeal mixture until combined. Stir in cheese and jalapeños. Carefully pour batter into hot oil. (Batter should sizzle.) Top with additional jalapeños, if desired.

3. Bake until golden brown and a wooden pick inserted in center comes out clean, 35 to 40 minutes. Serve immediately.

Cheese and Pepper Stuffed Cornbread

MAKES ABOUT 8 SERVINGS

A little heat and a lot of cheese pack this classic quick bread with extra flavor.

- **1 cup all-purpose flour**
- **1 cup plain yellow cornmeal**
- **½ teaspoon kosher salt**
- **½ teaspoon baking soda**
- **2 large eggs**
- **1 cup whole buttermilk**
- **½ cup unsalted butter, melted**
- **3 tablespoons honey**
- **2 cups shredded Monterey Jack cheese with peppers, divided**
- **¼ teaspoon crushed red pepper**

1. Preheat oven to 375°. Spray a 9-inch cast-iron skillet with cooking spray.

2. In a large bowl, stir together flour, cornmeal, salt, and baking soda. In a medium bowl, whisk together eggs, buttermilk, melted butter, and honey until smooth. Make a well in center of flour mixture; add egg mixture, stirring just until combined. Spread half of batter in prepared pan. Sprinkle with 1½ cups cheese. Spread remaining batter over cheese in an even layer. Do not stir. Sprinkle with red pepper and remaining ½ cup cheese.

3. Bake until golden brown, about 30 minutes. Let cool for 5 minutes before serving.

Straight from the Garden

Fresh produce as well as jarred and canned fruits and vegetables are an excellent way to dress up biscuits and quick breads. Use up any extras from your garden, the farmers' market, or your fridge in the process.

Sweet Potato and Ham Biscuits

MAKES 12

Southerners have long been enjoying a slice of country ham with their biscuits, so try a spin on this delightful pairing by incorporating it into the dough, giving each bite that perfect blend of salt and sweet heat.

4 cups self-rising flour
1 tablespoon firmly packed light brown sugar
½ teaspoon ground chipotle chile pepper
¼ teaspoon kosher salt
½ cup cold unsalted butter, cubed
1 cup finely diced country ham
1½ cups cold mashed cooked sweet potato
1 cup cold whole buttermilk
2 tablespoons unsalted butter, melted
Butter and syrup, to serve

1. In a large bowl, whisk together flour, brown sugar, chipotle, and salt. Using a pastry blender or 2 forks, cut in cold butter until mixture is crumbly and butter is the size of peas. Stir in ham.

2. In a small bowl, whisk together sweet potato and buttermilk; stir into flour mixture just until dry ingredients are moistened.

3. Turn out dough onto a lightly floured surface, and gently knead just until dough comes together, 4 to 6 times. Gently roll or pat dough to a 1-inch thickness. Using a 2½-inch round cutter dipped in flour, cut dough, without twisting cutter, into 12 biscuits, gently rerolling scraps as needed. Place biscuits in a 12-inch cast-iron skillet. Freeze for 15 minutes.

4. Preheat oven to 450°.

5. Bake until golden brown, 15 to 20 minutes. Brush with melted butter; serve warm with butter and syrup.

Chipotle Sweet Potato Biscuits

MAKES 9

Ground chipotle chiles give these sweet biscuits a hint of heat you won't be able to resist.

- **3 cups self-rising flour**
- **½ teaspoon sugar**
- **½ teaspoon ground chipotle chile pepper**
- **¼ teaspoon kosher salt**
- **½ cup cold unsalted butter, cubed**
- **1½ cups cold coarsely mashed cooked sweet potatoes (about 1¼ pounds)**
- **1 cup cold whole buttermilk**
- **2 teaspoons vegetable oil**
- **2 tablespoons unsalted butter, melted**

1. Preheat oven to 450°. Line a small baking sheet with parchment paper.

2. In a large bowl, whisk together flour, sugar, chipotle pepper, and salt. Using a pastry blender or 2 forks, cut in cold butter until mixture is crumbly and some pea-size pieces of butter remain.

3. In a small bowl, whisk together sweet potato and buttermilk; add to flour mixture, stirring just until dry ingredients are moistened.

4. On a floured surface, gently knead dough 4 to 6 times. Roll dough into an 8-inch square. Using a serrated knife dipped in flour, cut dough into 9 squares. Using a spatula, place biscuits on prepared pan. Place biscuits in freezer while cast-iron pan preheats.

5. Brush a 14-inch cast-iron baking pan with oil; place pan in oven until very hot, about 5 minutes. Remove biscuits from baking sheet, and place 1 inch apart on preheated pan.

6. Bake until golden brown, about 15 minutes. Brush with melted butter; serve warm.

Savory Green Tomato Cobbler

MAKES 6 TO 8 SERVINGS

Take this easy main-dish cobbler to your next potluck, family dinner, or gathering of any kind. It's sure to be a hit.

- **2 pounds green tomatoes, cut into 1-inch pieces (about 6½ cups)**
- **½ cup chopped fresh basil**
- **2 tablespoons cornstarch**
- **2½ teaspoons kosher salt, divided**
- **¾ teaspoon ground black pepper, plus more for sprinkling**
- **12 ounces thick-cut bacon, chopped**
- **1½ cups all-purpose flour**
- **2¼ teaspoons baking powder**
- **1½ tablespoons sugar**
- **½ cup shredded extra-sharp Cheddar cheese**
- **½ cup plus 1 tablespoon whole buttermilk, divided**
- **⅓ cup unsalted butter, melted**

1. Preheat oven to 350°.
2. In a large bowl, toss together tomatoes, basil, cornstarch, 1 teaspoon salt, and pepper.
3. In a 10-inch enamel-coated cast-iron skillet, cook bacon over medium-high heat until browned and crisp, about 10 minutes. Remove from pan using a slotted spoon, and let drain on paper towels, reserving 2 tablespoons drippings in pan.
4. Stir tomato mixture into pan; bring to a boil over medium heat. Reduce heat to medium-low; cook, stirring constantly, until tomatoes begin to soften, 5 to 7 minutes. Remove from heat.
5. In another large bowl, whisk together flour, baking powder, sugar, and remaining 1½ teaspoons salt; stir in cheese. Stir in ½ cup buttermilk and melted butter just until combined. Using a 3-tablespoon scoop, drop dough onto tomato mixture. Brush biscuits with remaining 1 tablespoon buttermilk. Sprinkle with pepper, if desired.
6. Bake until biscuits are golden brown and filling is bubbly, 25 to 30 minutes. Let stand for 10 to 15 minutes before serving.

Sun-Dried Tomato Muffins

MAKES 12

Packed with chewy sun-dried tomatoes that add a punch of tang, these quick muffins complement any weeknight dinner or Sunday supper.

- **3 cups all-purpose flour**
- **1½ tablespoons baking powder**
- **2 teaspoons kosher salt**
- **1 cup whole milk, room temperature**
- **½ cup mayonnaise**
- **¼ cup unsalted butter, melted and slightly cooled**
- **1 large egg, room temperature**
- **⅔ cup chopped oil-packed sun-dried tomatoes**

1. Preheat oven to 350°. Spray 2 (6-cup) cast-iron muffin pans with baking spray with flour.

2. In a large bowl, whisk together flour, baking powder, and salt. In a medium bowl, whisk together milk, mayonnaise, melted butter, and egg. Stir milk mixture into flour mixture just until dry ingredients are moistened; stir in tomatoes. Divide batter among prepared muffin cups (cups will be full).

3. Bake until a wooden pick inserted in center comes out clean, about 25 minutes. Let cool in pan on a wire rack for 10 minutes; serve warm.

Jalapeño-Cheese Puffs

MAKES ABOUT 30

A cross between a hush puppy and a muffin, these savory fried bites of goodness get taken to the next level thanks to a quintessential Southern ingredient: pimiento cheese.

Vegetable oil, for frying
3 cups all-purpose flour
¼ cup plain yellow cornmeal
2 tablespoons sugar
2 teaspoons baking powder
1 tablespoon kosher salt
½ teaspoon paprika
½ teaspoon ground black pepper
1 (12-ounce) container pimiento cheese*, room temperature, plus more for serving
2 large eggs
1 cup whole buttermilk, room temperature
¼ cup unsalted butter, melted
¼ cup minced seeded jalapeño

1. In a medium cast-iron Dutch oven, pour oil to a depth of 2 inches, and heat over medium heat until a deep-fry thermometer registers 325°.

2. In a medium bowl, whisk together flour, cornmeal, sugar, baking powder, salt, paprika, and black pepper. In a large bowl, whisk together pimiento cheese, eggs, buttermilk, and melted butter until well combined. Stir flour mixture into cheese mixture just until dry ingredients are moistened; stir in jalapeño until well combined.

3. Working in batches, using a 1½-tablespoon spring-loaded scoop, scoop dough into hot oil; fry, turning occasionally, until golden brown, 2 to 3 minutes. Remove using a slotted spoon, and let drain on paper towels. Serve warm with additional pimiento cheese.

**We used Pawleys Island Palmetto Cheese.*

Sour Cream and Onion Scones

MAKES 8

The popular potato chip flavoring was reimagined in these savory scones. You can cook these on a traditional baking sheet or in a large cast-iron skillet, but the cast-iron wedge pan helps give them wonderfully browned edges. Serve with herb butter, if you like.

- **2 cups all-purpose flour**
- **2 tablespoons ranch seasoning mix**
- **1 tablespoon baking powder**
- **¾ teaspoon kosher salt**
- **6 tablespoons cold unsalted butter, cubed**
- **¼ cup chopped green onion**
- **½ cup whole buttermilk, room temperature**
- **½ cup sour cream, room temperature**
- **1 egg, beaten**

1. Preheat oven to 400°. Spray an 8-well cast-iron wedge pan with baking spray with flour.
2. In a large bowl, whisk together flour, ranch mix, baking powder, and salt. Using a pastry blender or 2 forks, cut in cold butter until mixture is crumbly and butter is the size of peas. Stir in green onion.
3. In a small bowl, whisk together buttermilk and sour cream. Stir buttermilk mixture into flour mixture just until a shaggy dough forms.
4. Turn out dough onto a lightly floured surface, and gently knead dough just until it comes together. Pat dough into a 7-inch circle; cut into 8 wedges. Place wedges in wells of prepared pan. Brush egg onto wedges.
5. Bake until golden brown, 20 to 25 minutes. Let cool in pan on a wire rack for 5 minutes. Remove from pan, and let cool on a wire rack for 10 minutes. Serve warm.

Zucchini Bread with Buttermilk-Lemon Glaze

MAKES 1 (8X5-INCH) LOAF

The bountiful blessing (and curse!) of summer gardens, zucchini sneaks its way into many an old recipe, because no one wants to see it go to waste. This bread is one way to make a dent in your bumper crop.

- 2 cups all-purpose flour
- ¾ cup granulated sugar
- ½ cup toasted pecans, chopped
- 2 teaspoons baking powder
- ½ teaspoon baking soda
- ½ teaspoon ground nutmeg
- ½ teaspoon kosher salt
- 1 cup shredded zucchini (about 1 medium zucchini)
- ⅔ cup whole milk
- ⅓ cup unsalted butter, melted
- 2 teaspoons lemon zest
- 1 large egg
- ⅓ cup confectioners' sugar, sifted
- 2 teaspoons whole buttermilk
- 1 teaspoon fresh lemon juice

1. Preheat oven to 350°. Spray an 8x5-inch loaf pan with baking spray with flour.

2. In a large bowl, stir together flour, granulated sugar, pecans, baking powder, baking soda, nutmeg, and salt. Add zucchini, stirring to combine. In a small bowl, stir together milk, melted butter, lemon zest, and egg. Pour over flour mixture, stirring just until moistened. Spoon batter into prepared pan.

3. Bake until a wooden pick inserted in center comes out clean, about 50 minutes. Let cool in pan for 10 minutes. Remove from pan, and let cool completely on a wire rack.

4. In a small bowl, stir together confectioners' sugar, buttermilk, and lemon juice until smooth. Drizzle over bread.

Caramelized Vidalia Onion Bread

MAKES 1 (10-INCH) LOAF

Caramelizing onions takes a bit of patience, but they're easy to make, and their sweet flavor is worth the time.

¼ cup unsalted butter
8 cups (½-inch-thick) sliced Vidalia onion (about 2 pounds)
3 teaspoons chopped fresh thyme, divided
2¾ teaspoons kosher salt, divided
¾ teaspoon ground black pepper
4 cups all-purpose flour
1 tablespoon baking powder
1 teaspoon baking soda
2 cups whole buttermilk, room temperature
½ cup unsalted butter, melted
2 large eggs, room temperature
2 tablespoons firmly packed light brown sugar
½ cup shredded fontina cheese
Garnish: fresh thyme

1. Preheat oven to 350°.

2. In a 10-inch cast-iron skillet, heat butter over medium-high heat until bubbly. Add half of onion; cook, stirring frequently, until softened, 4 to 6 minutes. Add remaining onion; cook, stirring frequently, until softened, 4 to 6 minutes. Reduce heat to medium; cook, stirring frequently, until onions are lightly caramelized, 15 to 20 minutes.

3. Stir in 1 teaspoon thyme, 1 teaspoon salt, and pepper. Transfer onion mixture to a bowl. Wipe skillet clean, and spray with cooking spray.

4. In a large bowl, whisk together flour, baking powder, baking soda, remaining 2 teaspoons thyme, and remaining 1¾ teaspoons salt. In a medium bowl, whisk together buttermilk, melted butter, eggs, and brown sugar. Add buttermilk mixture to flour mixture, stirring just until combined. Finely chop ⅓ cup onion mixture, and gently fold into batter just until combined. Spread batter into prepared skillet; top with remaining onion mixture.

5. Bake until a wooden pick inserted in center comes out clean, 40 to 50 minutes, topping with cheese during last 5 minutes. Let cool for 15 minutes before serving. Garnish with thyme, if desired. Serve warm.

Heirloom Tomato and Parmesan Cornbread

MAKES 1 (10-INCH) LOAF

Showcase the seasonal sweetness and variety of heirloom tomatoes in this colorful cornbread.

3 small heirloom tomatoes, sliced ¼ inch thick and seeded
2 teaspoons kosher salt, divided
1 tablespoon canola oil
2 cups plain yellow cornmeal
1 cup all-purpose flour
1 tablespoon baking powder
2½ cups whole buttermilk
6 tablespoons unsalted butter, melted
2 large eggs
1 cup yellow corn kernels
½ cup chopped fresh basil
¾ cup grated Parmesan cheese, divided
Goat cheese, to serve
Garnish: fresh basil, ground black pepper

1. Place tomato slices on paper towels; sprinkle with ½ teaspoon salt. Let stand for 30 minutes.

2. Preheat oven to 425°.

3. Pour oil into a 10-inch cast-iron skillet. Place pan in oven until oil is very hot, about 8 minutes.

4. In a large bowl, whisk together cornmeal, flour, baking powder, and remaining 1½ teaspoons salt. In a medium bowl, whisk together buttermilk, melted butter, and eggs. Make a well in center of cornmeal mixture; stir in buttermilk mixture just until combined. Gently fold in corn, basil, and ½ cup Parmesan. Carefully pour batter into hot skillet.

5. Pat tomato slices dry, and arrange on top of batter. Sprinkle with remaining ¼ cup Parmesan.

6. Bake until golden brown and a wooden pick inserted in center comes out clean, about 55 minutes. Serve with goat cheese. Garnish with basil and pepper, if desired.

Spicy Sweet Potato Cornbread

MAKES 1 (10-INCH) LOAF

This moist, tender cornbread gets a hit of heat from the ground red pepper stirred into the batter. Don't be tempted to omit the spiced sorghum butter—it takes it over the top.

CORNBREAD

- 1 pound sweet potatoes, scrubbed well and pricked all over with a fork
- 2 tablespoons canola oil
- 2 cups plain yellow cornmeal
- 1 cup all-purpose flour
- 1 tablespoon baking powder
- 2 teaspoons kosher salt
- ¼ teaspoon baking soda
- ¼ teaspoon ground red pepper
- 2 large eggs
- 1½ cups whole buttermilk
- ½ cup unsalted butter, melted
- Spicy Sorghum Butter (recipe follows)

SPICY SORGHUM BUTTER

Makes ½ cup

- ½ cup unsalted butter, softened
- 2 tablespoons sorghum syrup, divided
- ¼ teaspoon kosher salt
- ⅛ teaspoon ground red pepper

For the Cornbread:

1. Microwave sweet potatoes on high until tender, 8 to 10 minutes, turning potatoes halfway through cooking. Carefully halve potatoes lengthwise, and let cool, cut side up. Peel potatoes, and mash pulp until smooth.
2. Preheat oven to 425°. Add oil to a 10-inch cast-iron skillet, and place skillet in oven until hot, about 5 minutes.
3. In a large bowl, whisk together cornmeal, flour, baking powder, salt, baking soda, and red pepper. In a medium bowl, whisk together 1 cup mashed sweet potato, eggs, buttermilk, and melted butter until well combined. Stir potato mixture into cornmeal mixture until combined.
4. Remove hot skillet from oven. Carefully spread batter into skillet.
5. Bake until golden brown and a wooden pick inserted in center comes out with a few moist crumbs attached, 25 to 30 minutes. Let cool in pan for 5 minutes. Serve hot with Spicy Sorghum Butter.

For the Butter:

1. In a small bowl, stir together butter, 1 tablespoon syrup, salt, and red pepper until smooth and well combined. Lightly swirl remaining 1 tablespoon syrup into butter mixture.

Upside-Down Tomato Cornbread

MAKES 1 (10-INCH) LOAF

Using heirloom tomatoes in this upside-down treat highlights their unique shapes; however, any large tomato will do. Using self-rising cornmeal mix eliminates or decreases the need for added leavening agents, simplifying the recipe.

CORNBREAD

- 2 tablespoons unsalted butter
- 2 tablespoons sugar
- 2 heirloom tomatoes, sliced into ½-inch-thick rounds
- 1½ cups Self-Rising Cornmeal Mix (recipe follows)
- ¾ cup grated Parmesan cheese
- 2 tablespoons chopped fresh dill
- ½ teaspoon ground black pepper
- ¼ teaspoon kosher salt
- ¾ cup plus 2 tablespoons whole buttermilk
- 5 tablespoons unsalted butter, melted
- 2 large eggs
- Garnish: chopped fresh dill, ground black pepper

SELF-RISING CORNMEAL MIX

Makes about 8 cups

- 6 cups blue, yellow, or white plain stone-ground cornmeal*
- 1½ cups all-purpose flour
- ½ cup baking powder
- 4 teaspoons kosher salt

For the Cornbread:

1. Preheat oven to 375°.
2. In a 10-inch cast-iron skillet, heat butter over medium heat until foamy; swirl to coat skillet. Sprinkle sugar into bottom of skillet. Add tomato slices, overlapping if necessary; cook for 1 minute. Remove from heat.
3. In a large bowl, whisk together Self-Rising Cornmeal Mix, cheese, dill, pepper, and salt. In a small bowl, whisk together buttermilk, melted butter, and eggs. Make a well in center of cornmeal mixture; stir in buttermilk mixture just until combined. Pour batter onto tomatoes.
4. Bake until a wooden pick inserted in center comes out clean, about 25 minutes. Let cool in pan for 10 minutes. Invert onto a serving platter. Garnish with dill and pepper, if desired. Serve warm.

For the Cornmeal Mix:

1. In a large bowl, whisk together all ingredients. Store in an airtight container (labeled with date) for up to 1 year.

**We used McEwen & Sons Stone Ground Cornmeal.*

Winter Farm Stand Cornbread

MAKES 1 (10-INCH) LOAF

Farmers' markets aren't just for summer. Load this masterpiece with all your winter harvest favorites for one pretty and delicious cornbread.

- 3 tablespoons plus ½ teaspoon canola oil, divided
- 2¼ cups chopped fresh kale, divided
- 2 cups plain yellow cornmeal
- 1 cup all-purpose flour
- 2¾ teaspoons kosher salt, divided
- 2 teaspoons garlic powder
- ½ teaspoon baking powder
- ½ teaspoon baking soda
- 2 cups whole buttermilk
- 2 large eggs, lightly beaten
- 3 tablespoons unsalted butter, melted
- 1 cup shredded extra-sharp Cheddar cheese, plus more for sprinkling
- 2 (4-ounce) jars diced pimientos, drained and divided
- ⅓ cup finely chopped jalapeño
- ½ small red onion, peeled and cut lengthwise into ¼-inch-thick wedges
- ½ cup halved pickled okra, patted dry
- 1 small jalapeño, stemmed and sliced into ¼-inch-thick rounds
- ¼ teaspoon ground black pepper

1. Preheat oven to 425°.

2. In a 10-inch cast-iron skillet, heat 1 tablespoon oil over medium heat. Add 2 cups kale; cook, stirring occasionally, until wilted and crisp-tender, 5 to 6 minutes. Transfer kale to a small bowl, and let cool for 10 minutes.

3. To skillet, add 2 tablespoons oil; place in oven until very hot, about 8 minutes.

4. In a large bowl, whisk together cornmeal, flour, 2½ teaspoons salt, garlic powder, baking powder, and baking soda. In another large bowl, whisk together buttermilk, eggs, and melted butter. Make a well in center of cornmeal mixture; whisk in buttermilk mixture just until combined. Stir in cooled kale, cheese, 1 jar pimientos, and chopped jalapeño. Carefully spread batter into hot skillet.

5. In a small bowl, toss together remaining ¼ cup kale and remaining ½ teaspoon oil. Sprinkle kale mixture, onion, okra, sliced jalapeño, and remaining jar of pimientos on top of batter. Sprinkle with black pepper and remaining ¼ teaspoon salt.

6. Bake until a wooden pick inserted in center comes out clean, 25 to 30 minutes, loosely covering with foil to prevent kale from overbrowning, if needed.

7. Sprinkle with additional cheese, if desired. Bake until cheese is melted, about 3 minutes more. Let cool in pan on a wire rack for 15 minutes before serving.

Caramelized Onion and Thyme Cornbread

MAKES 1 (10-INCH) LOAF

Every breadbasket needs a hearty cornbread in it, and this recipe has no shortage of deliciousness thanks to silky, sweet onions and fresh herbs along with crispy edges and a fluffy center.

8 tablespoons unsalted butter, divided
4 cups sliced yellow onion (about 2 medium onions)
2 cups plain yellow cornmeal
1 cup all-purpose flour
1½ tablespoons chopped fresh thyme
1 tablespoon baking powder
1½ teaspoons kosher salt
2½ cups whole buttermilk
2 large eggs
Garnish: fresh thyme

1. Preheat oven to 425°.
2. In a 10-inch cast-iron skillet, melt 2 tablespoons butter over medium heat. Add onion; cook, stirring occasionally, until soft and golden brown, 15 to 20 minutes. Reserve ½ cup onion in a small bowl. Transfer remaining onion to a medium bowl.
3. Wipe skillet clean. Add remaining 6 tablespoons butter to skillet, and place in oven until butter is melted and skillet is hot.
4. In a large bowl, whisk together cornmeal, flour, thyme, baking powder, and salt. In a small bowl, whisk together buttermilk and eggs. Stir buttermilk mixture into flour mixture just until dry ingredients are moistened; stir in onions.
5. Carefully pour melted butter into batter; stir until well combined. Spread batter into hot skillet; top with reserved onion.
6. Bake until golden brown and a wooden pick inserted in center comes out clean, 25 to 30 minutes. Let cool in pan on a wire rack for 5 minutes; serve hot. Garnish with thyme, if desired.

Southwestern Hoecakes

MAKES ABOUT 19

Also known as johnnycakes or corn cakes, these savory pancake-like delicacies can be enjoyed at any time of the day. Fire up your taste buds with our slightly spicy version that features a trifecta of peppers and then cool them back down with a dollop of dressed-up sour cream.

- 1 cup sour cream
- 2 tablespoons mayonnaise
- ⅛ teaspoon garlic powder
- ⅛ teaspoon onion powder
- ½ to ¾ cup plus 1 tablespoon vegetable oil, divided
- 1 cup diced assorted bell pepper
- ¼ cup diced seeded jalapeño
- 1 cup all-purpose flour
- 1 cup plain yellow cornmeal
- 1 tablespoon sugar
- 2 teaspoons baking powder
- 1½ teaspoons kosher salt
- ¼ teaspoon ground black pepper
- 2 large eggs
- ¾ cup whole buttermilk
- ½ cup water
- ¼ cup chopped fresh cilantro, plus more for garnish

1. In a small bowl, stir together sour cream, mayonnaise, garlic powder, and onion powder until smooth; cover and refrigerate.

2. In a large cast-iron skillet, heat 1 tablespoon oil over medium heat. Add bell pepper and jalapeño; cook, stirring occasionally, until browned and soft, about 7 minutes. Transfer vegetables to a small bowl.

3. In a medium bowl, whisk together flour, cornmeal, sugar, baking powder, salt, and black pepper. In a small bowl, whisk together eggs, buttermilk, ½ cup water, and ¼ cup oil until smooth. Stir egg mixture into flour mixture just until combined; stir in cooked vegetables and cilantro.

4. In same skillet, heat ¼ cup oil over medium heat. Drop batter by 2 tablespoonfuls into skillet; cook until golden brown, 1 to 2 minutes per side. Let drain briefly on paper towels. Repeat with remaining batter, using additional oil as needed. Serve warm with sour cream mixture. Garnish with cilantro, if desired.

Fun and Fruity

Adding colorful fruit to biscuits and quick breads transforms them into sweet treats for ordinary days or special occasions.

Pear-Ginger Biscuits

MAKES 8

A basket of these fluffy biscuits is a delicious way to welcome the morning. The creamy pear spread makes them extra special.

BISCUITS

- 3⅓ cups all-purpose flour
- ¼ cup plus 1 tablespoon sugar, divided
- 1 tablespoon baking powder
- ½ teaspoon baking soda
- ¾ teaspoon kosher salt
- ½ cup cold unsalted butter, cubed
- 1 cup diced peeled pear
- ¼ cup finely chopped crystallized ginger
- 1 teaspoon lemon zest (reserve lemon)
- 1¼ cups plus 1 tablespoon cold whole buttermilk, divided

SPREAD

- 1 (8-ounce) package cream cheese, softened
- ¼ cup pear preserves*
- 2 tablespoons fresh lemon juice (lemon reserved from biscuits)

For the Biscuits:

1. Preheat oven to 400°. Lightly spray a 14-inch cast-iron baking pan or baking sheet with cooking spray. In a large bowl, whisk together flour, ¼ cup sugar, baking powder, baking soda, and salt. Using a pastry blender or 2 forks, cut in cold butter until mixture is crumbly. Stir in pear, ginger, and zest. Using a fork, gradually stir in 1¼ cups buttermilk just until dry ingredients are moistened.

2. Turn out dough onto a lightly floured surface, and gently knead just until dough comes together, 4 to 5 times. Gently pat dough into a 12x6-inch rectangle, about ¾ inch thick. Using a sharp knife, cut dough into 8 (3-inch) squares. Place on prepared pan. Brush remaining 1 tablespoon buttermilk onto biscuits; sprinkle with remaining 1 tablespoon sugar.

3. Bake until golden brown, 20 to 25 minutes. Let cool on a wire rack for 5 minutes.

For the Spread:

1. In a small bowl, stir together cream cheese and preserves until well combined. Stir in lemon juice, 1 teaspoon at a time, as needed to reach a spreadable consistency. Serve with biscuits. Cover and refrigerate for up to 5 days.

**We used Braswell's Pure Pear Preserves.*

Strawberry Biscuits

MAKES ABOUT 11

Create strawberry shortcakes with these fluffy, golden-brown biscuits, tangy-sweet strawberry preserves, and a generous dollop of whipped cream.

3½ cups self-rising flour*
⅓ cup granulated sugar
¾ cup cold unsalted butter, cubed
¾ cup cold whole buttermilk
¾ cup chopped fresh strawberries
1 large egg, beaten
Sparkling sugar (optional)
Strawberry preserves and sweetened whipped cream, to serve

1. Preheat oven to 425°. Lightly spray a 12-inch cast-iron skillet with cooking spray.

2. In a large bowl, whisk together flour and granulated sugar. Using a pastry blender or 2 forks, cut in cold butter until mixture is crumbly. Stir in cold buttermilk and chopped strawberries until a shaggy dough forms.

3. Turn out dough onto a lightly floured surface. Pat dough into a rectangle, and cut into fourths. Stack each fourth on top of each other, and pat down into a rectangle again. Repeat process 3 more times.

4. Pat or roll dough to 1-inch thickness. Using a 2½-inch round cutter dipped in flour, cut dough without twisting cutter, rerolling scraps once. Place biscuits 2 inches apart in prepared pan. Freeze until cold, about 10 minutes. Brush beaten egg onto biscuits; sprinkle with sparkling sugar, if using.

5. Bake until golden brown, about 15 minutes. Let cool for 5 minutes. Serve with preserves and whipped cream. Store in an airtight container for up to 2 days.

**We used White Lily Self-Rising Flour.*

Peaches and Cream Shortcakes

MAKES 6

Simmered with vanilla and spices, peaches make an excellent filling for these sweet and crunchy brown sugar shortcakes.

BROWN SUGAR SHORTCAKES

- 1½ cups all-purpose flour
- ¼ cup firmly packed light brown sugar
- 2 teaspoons baking powder
- ¼ teaspoon kosher salt
- 4½ tablespoons cold unsalted butter, cubed
- ½ cup plus 2 tablespoons heavy whipping cream, divided
- ½ teaspoon vanilla extract
- 1 tablespoon granulated sugar

PEACH FILLING

- 2 (16-ounce) bags frozen peaches
- ½ cup firmly packed brown sugar
- ¼ cup heavy whipping cream
- ½ teaspoon ground cinnamon
- ½ teaspoon vanilla extract

Sweetened whipped cream
Garnish: toasted coconut

For the Shortcakes:

1. Preheat oven to 350°. Line a baking sheet with parchment paper. In a large bowl, whisk together flour, brown sugar, baking powder, and salt. Using a pastry blender or 2 forks, cut cold butter into flour mixture until crumbly. Make a well in flour mixture; add ½ cup cream and vanilla, stirring until mixture just comes together.

2. Turn out dough onto a lightly floured surface, and roll dough to a ½-inch thickness. Using a 3-inch round cutter dipped in flour, cut 6 biscuits without twisting cutter, rerolling scraps once. Place biscuits 2 inches apart on prepared pan. Brush tops with remaining 2 tablespoons cream, and sprinkle with granulated sugar. Bake until lightly browned, about 20 minutes.

For the Filling:

1. In a large saucepan, combine peaches, brown sugar, cream, cinnamon, and vanilla. Cook over medium-low heat until peaches are tender, about 10 minutes.

2. Cut Brown Sugar Shortcakes in half horizontally, and place bottom halves on 6 dessert plates. Spoon peach mixture over each half. Cover with top halves and whipped cream. Garnish with coconut, if desired.

Strawberry Shortcakes

MAKES 4 TO 5

Sometimes, simple really is best. This classic combination of strawberry biscuits, macerated fresh strawberries, and whipped cream is all the proof you need.

2 cups sliced fresh strawberries
¼ cup plus 2 tablespoons sugar, divided
2 teaspoons fresh lemon juice
¾ teaspoon plus ⅛ teaspoon kosher salt, divided
2 cups all-purpose flour
1 tablespoon baking powder
½ cup cold unsalted butter, cubed
¾ cup chopped fresh strawberries
1 cup whole milk
½ teaspoon vanilla extract
Sweetened whipped cream

1. In a medium bowl, toss together sliced strawberries, ¼ cup sugar, lemon juice, and ⅛ teaspoon salt. Let stand for at least 1 hour or up to 2 hours.

2. Preheat oven to 425°.

3. In a large bowl, whisk together flour, baking powder, remaining 2 tablespoons sugar, and remaining ¾ teaspoon salt. Using a pastry blender or 2 forks, cut in cold butter until mixture is crumbly. Pat chopped strawberries dry with a paper towel; add to flour mixture, tossing until combined. Gradually fold in milk and vanilla, folding until dry ingredients are moistened. (Dough will be sticky.)

4. On a floured surface, gently knead dough 4 to 5 times. Roll dough to ¾-inch thickness. Using a 3-inch round cutter dipped in flour, cut dough without twisting cutter, rerolling scraps once. Place 1 inch apart on a two-burner cast-iron griddle.

5. Bake until lightly browned, about 17 minutes. Let cool on pan for 5 minutes. Remove from pan, and let cool for 30 minutes on a wire rack. Halve shortcakes, and top with sliced strawberry mixture and whipped cream. Serve immediately.

Triple Berry Cobbler

MAKES 6 TO 8 SERVINGS

If you are in need of a patriotic-themed dessert that's easy to prepare, this cobbler meets the need. It's sure to be popular whenever you serve it.

3 cups fresh strawberries, quartered
3 cups fresh raspberries
3 cups fresh blueberries
1 cup plus 2 tablespoons granulated sugar, divided
¼ cup cornstarch
2 tablespoons fresh lemon juice
1 cup all-purpose flour
1½ teaspoons baking powder
¼ teaspoon kosher salt
3 tablespoons cold unsalted butter, cubed
⅔ cup whole milk
2 tablespoons coarse sugar
Homemade vanilla ice cream, to serve

1. Preheat oven to 375°.

2. In a large bowl, combine strawberries, raspberries, blueberries, 1 cup granulated sugar, cornstarch, and lemon juice. Spoon berry mixture into a 1½-quart baking dish.

3. In a medium bowl, whisk together flour, baking powder, remaining 2 tablespoons granulated sugar, and salt. Using a pastry blender or 2 forks, cut cold butter into flour mixture until crumbly. Make a well in flour mixture; add milk, stirring until mixture just comes together.

4. Bake fruit mixture for 10 minutes. Remove from oven. Using a 3-tablespoon scoop, drop dough over fruit. Sprinkle with coarse sugar. Bake until biscuits are golden brown and fruit is bubbly, 35 to 40 minutes more. Serve with ice cream.

Blackberry Cobbler

MAKES 12 SERVINGS

When it comes to cooking, sometimes, it's OK to cheat a little bit. Frozen biscuits can be a huge time-saver, and while they're not quite as perfect as homemade, they'll do in a pinch.

9 cups fresh blackberries
1 cup plus 1 tablespoon sugar, divided
6 tablespoons all-purpose flour
1 (24-ounce) package frozen bite-size buttermilk tea biscuits*
1 tablespoon unsalted butter, melted
¼ teaspoon ground cinnamon

1. Preheat oven to 350°.

2. In a large bowl, combine blackberries, 1 cup sugar, and flour. Spoon into a 13x9-inch baking dish. Bake for 20 minutes. Remove from oven.

3. Place biscuits on a baking sheet. Bake for 10 minutes. Remove biscuits from baking sheet, and place on blackberry mixture. Brush biscuits with melted butter.

4. In a small bowl, combine cinnamon and remaining 1 tablespoon sugar. Sprinkle over biscuits.

5. Bake until browned and bubbly, about 20 minutes.

**We used Mary B's.*

Fresh Cherry-Almond Cobbler

MAKES 6 TO 8 SERVINGS

Fresh cherries are such a treat. Serve this with a generous scoop of vanilla ice cream and an extra sprinkle of toasted almonds.

2½ pounds pitted fresh cherries (about 5 cups)
1 cup granulated sugar, divided
1 cup all-purpose flour, divided
2 tablespoons fresh lemon juice
¼ teaspoon almond extract
½ cup almond flour
1 teaspoon kosher salt
¾ teaspoon baking powder
6 tablespoons cold unsalted butter, cubed
½ cup whole buttermilk
Garnish: sliced toasted almonds, confectioners' sugar

1. Preheat oven to 350°.

2. In a large bowl, stir together cherries, ¾ cup granulated sugar, ¼ cup all-purpose flour, lemon juice, and almond extract. Spoon cherry mixture into a 2-quart baking dish.

3. In a medium bowl, whisk together remaining ¾ cup all-purpose flour, almond flour, remaining ¼ cup granulated sugar, salt, and baking powder. Using a pastry blender or 2 forks, cut cold butter into flour mixture until crumbly. Make a well in flour mixture; add buttermilk, stirring until mixture just comes together. (Dough will be wet.) Drop dough over cherry mixture.

4. Bake until browned and bubbly, 40 to 50 minutes. Let cool for 10 minutes. Garnish with almonds and confectioners' sugar, if desired.

Homestyle Peach Cobbler

MAKES 8 SERVINGS

There are two camps when it comes to cobbler—those who crave more fruit and those who demand more topping. Topping lovers, this one is for you. The extra fat from the whipping cream allows the topping to spread, baking into a sweet blanket of biscuit goodness.

- **5 cups sliced peeled fresh peaches or 2 (20-ounce) packages frozen sliced peaches, thawed**
- **1½ cups granulated sugar, divided**
- **1½ cups all-purpose flour, divided**
- **1 teaspoon almond extract**
- **1½ teaspoons baking powder**
- **¾ teaspoon kosher salt**
- **6 tablespoons cold unsalted butter, cubed**
- **½ cup heavy whipping cream**
- **1 tablespoon white sparkling sugar**

1. Preheat oven to 350°.

2. In a 2½-quart baking dish, combine peaches, 1 cup granulated sugar, ¼ cup flour, and almond extract.

3. In a medium bowl, whisk together remaining 1¼ cups flour, remaining ½ cup granulated sugar, baking powder, and salt. Using a pastry blender or 2 forks, cut cold butter into flour mixture until crumbly. Make a well in flour mixture; add cream, stirring until mixture just comes together.

4. Tear dough into 3-inch round pieces; arrange over peach mixture. Sprinkle with sparkling sugar.

5. Bake until browned and bubbly, 35 to 40 minutes. Let cool for 10 minutes before serving.

Strawberry Cobbler

MAKES 6 TO 8 SERVINGS

This skillet version of strawberry shortcake is a simple yet showstopping dessert. Be sure to use an enamel-coated cast-iron skillet to ensure the strawberry filling is ruby red and delicious.

FILLING

- 6 cups quartered fresh strawberries (about 2 pounds)
- 1 cup granulated sugar
- ¼ cup cornstarch
- 1 teaspoon lime zest
- 1 tablespoon fresh lime juice
- ½ teaspoon ground cinnamon
- ¼ teaspoon kosher salt
- 1 large egg

BISCUIT TOPPING

- 2 cups self-rising flour
- ⅓ cup plain cornmeal
- ⅓ cup granulated sugar
- ½ cup cold unsalted butter, cubed
- ⅔ cup whole buttermilk
- 1 tablespoon coarse sugar

Vanilla ice cream, to serve

For the Filling:

1. Preheat oven to 350°. Spray a 10-inch enamel-coated cast-iron skillet with cooking spray. In a large bowl, stir together strawberries, granulated sugar, cornstarch, lime zest and juice, cinnamon, salt, and egg. Transfer to prepared skillet.

For the Topping:

1. In a medium bowl, whisk together flour, cornmeal, and granulated sugar. Using a pastry blender or 2 forks, cut cold butter into flour mixture until crumbly. Make a well in flour mixture; add buttermilk, stirring until mixture just comes together. Drop 3-inch pieces of dough over strawberry filling. Sprinkle with coarse sugar.

2. Bake until browned and bubbly, 45 to 50 minutes, loosely covering with foil to prevent excess browning, if necessary. Serve with ice cream.

Individual Nectarine and Raspberry Cobblers

MAKES 8

Dessert's just a little more fun when you get your very own personal dish that you don't have to share! Feel free to mix up the fruit—switch out the nectarines for plums or peaches, if you like.

- **⅔ cup plus 4 tablespoons sugar, divided**
- **¼ cup cornstarch**
- **1½ teaspoons lemon zest**
- **4 cups peeled, pitted, and sliced fresh nectarines (about 8 nectarines)**
- **3 (6-ounce) containers fresh raspberries**
- **1½ cups all-purpose flour**
- **1½ teaspoons baking powder**
- **½ teaspoon kosher salt**
- **1½ cups heavy whipping cream**

1. Preheat oven to 400°.
2. In a small bowl, combine ⅔ cup sugar, cornstarch, and zest.
3. In a large bowl, toss together nectarines, raspberries, and sugar mixture until fruit is evenly coated. Divide fruit among 8 (6- to 8-ounce) ramekins.
4. In a medium bowl, whisk together flour, 2 tablespoons sugar, baking powder, and salt. Pour cream into flour mixture, and stir with a wooden spoon just until combined. Divide dough among ramekins, placing on top of fruit mixture. Sprinkle dough with remaining 2 tablespoons sugar.
5. Bake until biscuits are golden brown and fruit is bubbly, about 25 minutes. Let cool slightly before serving.

Lemon Poppy Seed Muffins

MAKES 12

The citrus-scented sugar on top of these muffins melts just enough while baking to add a sweet finishing crunch.

- **1¼ cups all-purpose flour**
- **⅔ cup firmly packed light brown sugar**
- **1 tablespoon poppy seeds**
- **¾ teaspoon baking powder**
- **½ teaspoon kosher salt**
- **¼ teaspoon baking soda**
- **½ cup whole buttermilk**
- **¼ cup unsalted butter, melted**
- **4 teaspoons lemon zest, divided**
- **1 teaspoon vanilla extract**
- **1 large egg**
- **¼ cup granulated sugar**

1. Preheat oven to 350°. Spray 2 (6-cup) cast-iron muffin pans with baking spray with flour.

2. In a large bowl, whisk together flour, brown sugar, poppy seeds, baking powder, salt, and baking soda. In a medium bowl, whisk together buttermilk, melted butter, 3 teaspoons lemon zest, vanilla, and egg. Whisk buttermilk mixture into flour mixture until combined. Divide batter among prepared muffin cups.

3. In a small bowl, whisk together granulated sugar and remaining 1 teaspoon lemon zest; sprinkle mixture onto batter.

4. Bake until a wooden pick inserted in center comes out clean, 18 to 20 minutes. Let cool in pans for 10 minutes. Serve warm, or remove from pans, and let cool completely on a wire rack.

Blueberry-Sweet Potato Scones

MAKES 8

Roasted sweet potatoes and blueberries add natural sweetness and vibrant color to these easy-to-bake scones.

- **2 cups all-purpose flour**
- **¼ cup granulated sugar**
- **1 tablespoon baking powder**
- **1 teaspoon ground cinnamon**
- **½ teaspoon kosher salt**
- **½ teaspoon grated fresh nutmeg**
- **½ cup cold unsalted butter, cubed**
- **1 cup mashed roasted sweet potato**
- **⅔ cup plus 1 teaspoon cold heavy whipping cream, divided**
- **¾ cup frozen blueberries, divided**
- **1 large egg**
- **1 cup confectioners' sugar**
- **½ cup maple syrup**

1. Preheat oven to 425°. Line a 14-inch round cast-iron baking pan with parchment paper.

2. In the work bowl of a food processor, pulse together flour, granulated sugar, baking powder, cinnamon, salt, and nutmeg until combined. Add cold butter, and pulse until mixture is crumbly. Transfer mixture to a medium bowl; stir in mashed sweet potato and ⅔ cup cream just until combined.

3. Turn out dough onto a lightly floured surface, and knead just until dough comes together. Pat dough to ½-inch thickness. Sprinkle ½ cup blueberries on top. Fold dough in half, and shape into an 8-inch circle. Sprinkle remaining ¼ cup blueberries on top of dough, gently pressing into dough. Using a sharp knife or bench scraper, cut dough into 8 wedges. Transfer wedges to prepared pan.

4. In a small bowl, whisk together egg and remaining 1 teaspoon cream; brush onto scones.

5. Bake until golden brown, 20 to 25 minutes. Let cool on a wire rack for 5 minutes.

6. In another small bowl, whisk together confectioners' sugar and syrup until smooth; drizzle onto warm scones.

Peach Scones

MAKES 8

If you have a love for biscuit-topped summer peach cobbler, you'll appreciate these delicious scones drizzled with a vanilla glaze.

- **2¼ cups all-purpose flour**
- **½ cup granulated sugar**
- **2 teaspoons baking powder**
- **½ teaspoon kosher salt**
- **¼ teaspoon baking soda**
- **¼ teaspoon ground nutmeg**
- **½ cup unsalted butter, frozen**
- **1 cup whole buttermilk**
- **1¼ teaspoons vanilla extract, divided**
- **1 large egg**
- **½ cup finely chopped peeled fresh peaches**
- **1½ cups confectioners' sugar**
- **3 tablespoons whole milk**

1. Preheat oven to 400°. Spray an 8-well cast-iron wedge pan with cooking spray.
2. In a large bowl, whisk together flour, granulated sugar, baking powder, salt, baking soda, and nutmeg; make a well in center of flour mixture. Grate frozen butter into flour mixture; gently stir just until combined.
3. In a medium bowl, whisk together buttermilk, 1 teaspoon vanilla, and egg until smooth. Add buttermilk mixture to flour mixture, stirring until mixture forms a shaggy dough. Gently stir in peaches.
4. On a heavily floured surface, knead mixture until it comes together, about 5 times. Gently pat and shape dough into a 7-inch circle. Cut into 8 wedges, and place in prepared wells.
5. Bake until golden brown and wooden pick inserted in center comes out clean, 18 to 20 minutes. Let cool in pan for 10 minutes.
6. In a small bowl, whisk together confectioners' sugar, milk, and remaining ¼ teaspoon vanilla until smooth; drizzle onto warm scones before serving.

Classic Banana Bread

MAKES 1 (9-INCH) LOAF

Try toasting a slice of this comforting quick bread in a buttered skillet for a breakfast treat.

1/3 cup whole buttermilk
1 teaspoon baking soda
1/2 cup unsalted butter, softened
1 cup sugar
2 large eggs
2 1/4 cups all-purpose flour
1/2 teaspoon kosher salt
1/2 teaspoon ground cinnamon
1/4 teaspoon ground nutmeg
1 1/2 cups mashed banana (about 3 medium bananas)
1 teaspoon vanilla extract

1. Preheat oven to 325°. Spray bottom only of a 9-inch loaf pan with baking spray with flour.

2. In a small bowl, stir together buttermilk and baking soda; let stand for 5 minutes.

3. In a large bowl, beat butter and sugar with a mixer at medium speed until fluffy, 3 to 4 minutes, stopping to scrape sides of bowl. Add eggs, one at a time, beating well after each addition.

4. In a medium bowl, whisk together flour, salt, cinnamon, and nutmeg. With mixer on low speed, gradually add flour mixture, buttermilk mixture, and banana to butter mixture. Beat in vanilla. Spoon batter into prepared pan, smoothing top with an offset spatula.

5. Bake until a wooden pick inserted in center comes out clean, about 1 hour and 10 minutes. Let cool in pan for 10 minutes. Remove from pan, and let cool completely on a wire rack.

Blackberry-Zucchini Bread

MAKES 1 (10-INCH) LOAF

Using a skillet for this stir-together quick bread makes for a shorter baking time than using a traditional loaf pan, creating a more tender crust and guarding against mushy berries.

2 cups shredded zucchini
1¼ cups plus 1 tablespoon granulated sugar, divided
2 cups self-rising flour
¼ cup self-rising yellow cornmeal
½ teaspoon kosher salt
¾ cup whole buttermilk
½ cup unsalted butter, melted
½ teaspoon vanilla extract
2 large eggs
1 cup halved fresh blackberries
Garnish: confectioners' sugar

1. In a fine-mesh strainer, toss together zucchini and 1 tablespoon granulated sugar. Let drain for 1 hour. Squeeze dry.

2. Preheat oven to 350°. Spray a 10-inch cast-iron skillet with baking spray with flour.

3. In a large bowl, whisk together flour, cornmeal, and salt. In another large bowl, whisk together zucchini, ¾ cup granulated sugar, buttermilk, melted butter, vanilla, and eggs. Pour zucchini mixture onto flour mixture, and stir just until combined. Spread batter into prepared skillet.

4. In a small bowl, toss together blackberries and remaining ½ cup granulated sugar. Sprinkle onto batter. Using the tip of a knife, swirl blackberries into batter.

5. Bake until edges are lightly browned and a wooden pick inserted in center comes out clean, 45 to 50 minutes. Let cool completely in pan. Garnish with confectioners' sugar, if desired.

Easy Lemon Bread

MAKES 1 (9X5-INCH) LOAF

Because quick breads are so easy, it's tempting to throw everything but the kitchen sink into the bowl. This recipe is divinely simple, accented with the sweet tartness of fresh lemon.

- **½ cup unsalted butter, softened**
- **1¼ cups sugar, divided**
- **2 large eggs**
- **1¼ cups all-purpose flour**
- **1 teaspoon double-acting baking powder**
- **¼ teaspoon kosher salt**
- **½ cup whole milk**
- **1 teaspoon lemon zest**
- **¼ cup fresh lemon juice**

1. Preheat oven to 350°. Spray a 9x5-inch loaf pan with baking spray with flour.

2. In a large bowl, beat butter and 1 cup sugar with a mixer at medium speed until fluffy, 3 to 4 minutes, stopping to scrape sides of bowl. Add eggs, one at time, beating well after each addition.

3. In a medium bowl, sift together flour, baking powder, and salt. Gradually add flour mixture to butter mixture alternately with milk, beginning and ending with flour mixture, beating just until combined after each addition. Stir in zest. Pour batter into prepared pan.

4. Bake until a wooden pick inserted in center comes out clean, about 1 hour. Place pan on a wire rack. Using a wooden skewer, poke holes in bread.

5. In a small bowl, combine lemon juice and remaining ¼ cup sugar. Pour mixture over hot bread. Let cool completely in pan.

Skillet Blackberry Bread

MAKES 1 (10-INCH) LOAF

Swirls of delicious blackberry jam give this easy-to-make skillet bread just the right amount of sweetness.

2 cups self-rising flour
½ teaspoon ground cardamom
¼ teaspoon kosher salt
1 (13-ounce) jar peach preserves
¾ cup unsalted butter, melted
¾ cup whole buttermilk
2 teaspoons vanilla extract
3 large eggs
⅔ cup blackberry jam
2 teaspoons sugar

1. Preheat oven to 350°. Spray a 10-inch cast-iron skillet with baking spray with flour.

2. In a large bowl, stir together flour, cardamom, and salt. In a medium bowl, whisk together peach preserves, melted butter, buttermilk, vanilla, and eggs. Make a well in center of flour mixture. Add preserves mixture, stirring just until dry ingredients are moistened. Pour batter into prepared skillet. Spoon blackberry jam over batter. Using the tip of a knife, gently swirl jam into batter.

3. Bake until a wooden pick inserted in center comes out clean, 35 to 40 minutes. Sprinkle sugar over hot bread. Let cool completely before slicing.

Nectarine Cornmeal Loaf with Lemon-Thyme Syrup

MAKES 1 (8-INCH) LOAF

Slice into this loaf and taste how bright citrus and fresh herb flavors balance the sweetness of juicy nectarines.

1½ cups all-purpose flour
1 cup sugar, divided
2 tablespoons plain yellow cornmeal
1½ teaspoons baking powder
¼ teaspoon kosher salt
⅛ teaspoon ground cinnamon
2 large eggs
¼ cup whole milk
¼ cup unsalted butter, melted
1 teaspoon vanilla extract
1 teaspoon lemon zest, divided
1 cup chopped pitted fresh nectarines
6 (¼-inch-thick) slices nectarine
¼ cup water
2 large sprigs fresh thyme
Garnish: fresh thyme sprigs

1. Preheat oven to 325°. Spray an 8½x4½-inch cast-iron loaf pan with baking spray with flour.

2. In a large bowl, whisk together flour, ¾ cup sugar, cornmeal, baking powder, salt, and cinnamon. In a medium bowl, whisk together eggs, milk, melted butter, vanilla, and ¾ teaspoon zest. Add milk mixture to flour mixture, and beat with a mixer at low speed just until combined. Gently stir in chopped nectarines. Spread batter into prepared pan. Place sliced nectarines about ¼ inch apart on top of batter.

3. Bake until a wooden pick inserted in center comes out clean, about 55 minutes, loosely covering with foil during last 10 minutes of baking to prevent excess browning, if necessary. Let cool in pan on a wire rack for 20 minutes. Run a knife around edges of bread. Remove from pan, and let cool completely on a wire rack.

4. In a small saucepan, bring ¼ cup water and remaining ¼ cup sugar to a boil over medium-high heat, stirring occasionally, until sugar is dissolved. Add thyme and remaining ¼ teaspoon zest, remove from heat, and let cool completely. Discard thyme before using.

5. Drizzle Lemon-Thyme Syrup onto cooled loaf. Garnish with thyme, if desired. Store in an airtight container for up to 3 days.

Spice and Everything Nice

Spices, herbs, and other flavorful additions are an easy way to make biscuits and quick breads even more extraordinary. These recipes share a variety of options to suit whatever you're craving.

Pecan and Goat Cheese Biscuits

MAKES 16

The tangy goat cheese and woodsy thyme flavors meld so beautifully in these little dinner biscuits, and the pecans add a perfect, hearty crunch. Pair them with roasted chicken or pork tenderloin.

4 cups self-rising flour
1 teaspoon kosher salt
¾ cup cold unsalted butter, cubed
1½ cups pecans, chopped
6 ounces crumbled goat cheese, chilled
2 teaspoons chopped fresh thyme
1¾ cups whole buttermilk
2 tablespoons unsalted butter, melted
Cane syrup, to serve

1. Preheat oven to 425°. Spray a 12-inch cast-iron skillet with cooking spray.

2. In a large bowl, whisk together flour and salt. Using a pastry blender or 2 forks, cut cold butter into flour mixture until crumbly. Stir in pecans, goat cheese, and thyme. Make a well in flour mixture; add buttermilk, stirring until mixture just comes together. Using a 4-tablespoon scoop, drop into prepared skillet. Brush with melted butter.

3. Bake until tops are golden, 30 to 35 minutes, loosely covering with foil to prevent excess browning, if necessary. Serve with cane syrup.

Snickerdoodle Biscuits

MAKES 8

If cinnamon toast was a staple in your house on Saturday mornings, then these biscuits will take you right back there. The sweet and crunchy cinnamon-sugar topping is better than hours of uninterrupted cartoons.

2 cups all-purpose flour
1 tablespoon baking powder
1 tablespoon plus ½ teaspoon sugar, divided
¾ teaspoon kosher salt
½ cup cold unsalted butter, cubed
1 cup whole buttermilk, divided
1 tablespoon unsalted butter, melted
½ teaspoon ground cinnamon
Strawberry preserves, to serve

1. Preheat oven to 425°.

2. In a large bowl, whisk together flour, baking powder, ½ teaspoon sugar, and salt. Using a pastry blender or 2 forks, cut cold butter into flour mixture until crumbly. Make a well in flour mixture; add ¾ cup buttermilk, stirring until mixture just comes together. (Add remaining ¼ cup buttermilk, if necessary.)

3. On a lightly floured surface, gently knead dough 4 or 5 times. Roll dough to ¾-inch thickness. Brush dough with melted butter.

4. In a small bowl, combine remaining 1 tablespoon sugar and cinnamon. Sprinkle half of cinnamon mixture over dough. Fold dough in half; roll to ¾-inch thickness. Using a 2½-inch round cutter dipped in flour, cut 8 biscuits without twisting cutter, rerolling scraps once. Place biscuits in a 12-inch cast-iron skillet or on a parchment-lined baking sheet. Sprinkle with remaining cinnamon mixture.

5. Bake until lightly browned, about 17 minutes. Serve with preserves.

Gingerbread Biscuits

MAKES ABOUT 12

Warm, fluffy biscuits should always have a place on your breakfast table, so start off the morning right with a big batch of these spice-infused beauties.

- 3½ cups all-purpose flour
- 1 tablespoon firmly packed light brown sugar
- 1 tablespoon kosher salt, plus more for sprinkling if desired
- 1 tablespoon baking powder
- 2½ teaspoons ground ginger, divided
- 2 teaspoons ground cinnamon, divided
- ½ teaspoon baking soda
- ½ teaspoon ground cloves, divided
- ¼ teaspoon ground nutmeg
- 1¼ cups cold unsalted butter, cubed
- 1 cup cold whole buttermilk
- 2½ tablespoons unsulphured molasses, divided
- 1 large egg, lightly beaten
- ½ cup unsalted butter, softened

1. In a large bowl, whisk together flour, brown sugar, 1 tablespoon salt, baking powder, 1½ teaspoons ginger, 1½ teaspoons cinnamon, baking soda, ¼ teaspoon cloves, and nutmeg. Using a pastry blender or 2 forks, cut in cold butter until mixture is crumbly.

2. In a small bowl, whisk together buttermilk and 1½ tablespoons molasses; stir into flour mixture until a shaggy dough forms.

3. Turn out dough onto a lightly floured surface. Pat dough into a 10x8-inch rectangle, and cut into fourths. Stack each fourth on top of each other, and pat or roll into a rectangle again. Repeat process three more times. Pat or roll dough to ¾-inch thickness. Using a 2½-inch round cutter dipped in flour, cut dough without twisting cutter, rerolling scraps as necessary. Place biscuits on a parchment-lined baking sheet. Freeze until cold, about 10 minutes.

4. Preheat oven to 400°.

5. Lightly brush egg onto biscuits; lightly sprinkle salt onto biscuits, if desired. Place biscuits, sides touching, in a 12-inch cast-iron skillet or ½ inch apart on a 15-inch cast-iron baking sheet.

6. Bake until golden brown, 15 to 17 minutes. Let cool on pan for 5 minutes.

7. In a medium bowl, stir together softened butter, 1 tablespoon molasses, 1 teaspoon ginger, ½ teaspoon cinnamon, and ¼ teaspoon cloves until well combined. Serve biscuits warm with butter mixture. Refrigerate butter mixture in an airtight container for up to 1 week.

Chocolate Chip Biscuits

MAKES 9

The whipping cream glaze and chocolate chips are the perfect decadent additions that are just sweet enough.

- 2 cups all-purpose flour
- 1 tablespoon baking powder
- 1 tablespoon granulated sugar
- ¾ teaspoon plus ⅛ teaspoon kosher salt, divided
- ½ cup cold unsalted butter, cubed
- ½ cup semisweet chocolate morsels
- 1 cup whole buttermilk, divided
- 1 cup confectioners' sugar
- ⅓ cup heavy whipping cream
- ¼ teaspoon vanilla extract

1. Preheat oven to 425°.

2. In a large bowl, whisk together flour, baking powder, granulated sugar, and ¾ teaspoon salt. Using a pastry blender or 2 forks, cut cold butter into flour mixture until crumbly. Add chocolate morsels, tossing until combined. Make a well in flour mixture; add ¾ cup buttermilk, stirring until mixture just comes together. Add remaining ¼ cup buttermilk, if necessary.

3. On a lightly floured surface, gently knead dough 4 or 5 times. Roll dough to ¾-inch thickness. Fold dough in half; roll dough to ¾-inch thickness. Using a 2½-inch round cutter dipped in flour, cut 9 biscuits without twisting cutter, rerolling scraps once. Place biscuits in a 10-inch cast-iron skillet, touching slightly, or on a parchment-lined baking sheet.

4. Bake until lightly browned, about 17 minutes. Let cool in pan for 30 minutes.

5. In a small bowl, stir together confectioners' sugar, cream, vanilla, and remaining ⅛ teaspoon salt. Drizzle biscuits with cream glaze.

Chocolate Biscuits with Chocolate Gravy

MAKES ABOUT 12

Who says you can't have chocolate for breakfast? These warm, cake-like biscuits are pretty perfect drizzled with Chocolate Gravy.

BISCUITS

- 1 tablespoon canola oil
- 2½ cups all-purpose flour
- ¾ cup granulated sugar
- ⅔ cup unsweetened cocoa powder
- ½ cup semisweet chocolate morsels
- 4 teaspoons baking powder
- ½ teaspoon baking soda
- ½ teaspoon kosher salt
- ¾ cup cold unsalted butter, cubed
- 1 cup whole milk
- 2 teaspoons vanilla extract
- ¾ cup semisweet chocolate chunks
- Chocolate Gravy (recipe follows), to serve

CHOCOLATE GRAVY

Makes about 2¼ cups

- ½ cup firmly packed light brown sugar
- ¼ cup unsweetened cocoa powder
- 2 tablespoons all-purpose flour
- ⅛ teaspoon kosher salt
- 2 cups whole milk
- 3 tablespoons semisweet chocolate morsels
- ½ teaspoon vanilla extract

For the Biscuits:

1. Preheat oven to 425°. Brush a 12-inch cast-iron skillet with oil. Place in oven until very hot, about 8 minutes.
2. In a large bowl, whisk together flour, granulated sugar, cocoa, chocolate morsels, baking powder, baking soda, and salt. Using a pastry blender or 2 forks, cut in cold butter until mixture is crumbly. Gradually add milk and vanilla, stirring just until dry ingredients are moistened.
3. On a lightly floured surface, gently knead dough 4 times. Roll dough to a ¾-inch thickness. Using a 3-inch round cutter, cut dough without twisting cutter, rerolling scraps once. Carefully place in hot pan, overlapping slightly.
4. Bake until tops feel set and biscuits are cooked through, about 22 minutes. Sprinkle chocolate chunks over hot biscuits. Let cool in pan for 10 minutes. Serve warm with Chocolate Gravy.

For the Gravy:

1. In a large saucepan, whisk together brown sugar, cocoa, flour, and salt; whisk in milk. Bring to a simmer over medium heat, whisking constantly. Reduce heat; simmer until thickened and bubbly, about 2 minutes. Remove from heat. Add chocolate morsels and vanilla, stirring until chocolate melts.

Spiced Apple Shortcakes

MAKES 4 SERVINGS

This one-skillet dessert makes for easy cleanup. To prep ahead, bake the shortcakes earlier in the day and make the quick apple filling and whipped cream just before serving.

SHORTCAKES

- 2 cups self-rising flour
- ⅓ cup granulated sugar
- ½ teaspoon ground cinnamon
- ¼ teaspoon ground ginger
- 6 tablespoons cold unsalted butter, cubed
- ⅓ cup plus 2 tablespoons whole buttermilk, divided
- 1 large egg
- 1 teaspoon vanilla extract
- 1 tablespoon heavy whipping cream

FILLING

- 2 tablespoons unsalted butter
- 2 cups sliced peeled Golden Delicious apples
- 2 cups sliced peeled Gala apples
- ⅓ cup firmly packed light brown sugar
- ½ teaspoon ground cinnamon
- ⅛ teaspoon ground cloves
- ⅛ teaspoon kosher salt
- ½ teaspoon lemon zest

Bourbon Whipped Cream (recipe follows)

BOURBON WHIPPED CREAM

Makes about 2 cups

- 1 cup cold heavy whipping cream
- 3 tablespoons firmly packed light brown sugar
- 2 tablespoons bourbon
- ¼ teaspoon ground cinnamon

For the Shortcakes:

1. Preheat oven to 425°. In a large bowl, whisk together flour, granulated sugar, cinnamon, and ginger. Using a pastry blender or 2 forks, cut in cold butter until mixture is crumbly. In a small bowl, whisk together ⅓ cup buttermilk, egg, and vanilla. Make a well in center of flour mixture; add buttermilk mixture, stirring just until combined. Add remaining 2 tablespoons buttermilk, if necessary.

2. Turn out dough onto a lightly floured surface. Using floured hands, pat dough to ¾-inch thickness. Using a 3-inch round cutter, cut 4 rounds without twisting cutter. Place on a parchment-lined small baking sheet. Freeze for 10 minutes. Place dough rounds in a 10-inch cast-iron skillet. Brush with cream.

3. Bake until golden brown, about 18 minutes. Let cool in pan for 5 minutes. Remove from pan, and let cool on a wire rack.

For the Filling:

1. In a cast-iron skillet, melt butter over medium-high heat. Reduce heat to medium. Add apples, brown sugar, cinnamon, cloves, and salt; cook, stirring frequently, until lightly browned and softened, 5 to 7 minutes. Stir in zest, and remove from heat. Halve shortcakes, and fill with apple mixture. Serve with Bourbon Whipped Cream.

For the Whipped Cream:

1. In a medium bowl, beat all ingredients with a mixer at high speed until stiff peaks form. Serve immediately.

Rosemary Shortcakes with Apple-Plum Sauce

MAKES 4

These aren't your grandmother's shortcakes. This twist on the classic is fun to serve guests. The flavor combination is unexpected, and the recipe is easy to make ahead of time.

SHORTCAKES

- 2 cups self-rising flour
- 2½ tablespoons granulated sugar
- 1 teaspoon finely chopped fresh rosemary
- ¼ teaspoon kosher salt
- ½ cup unsalted butter, softened
- ¼ cup whole milk
- 2 tablespoons heavy whipping cream

APPLE-PLUM SAUCE

- 1 cup water
- ⅔ cup granulated sugar
- ¼ cup red wine vinegar
- 3 plums, peeled and sliced
- 1 Granny Smith apple, peeled and sliced
- 1 teaspoon orange zest

WHIPPED CREAM

- 1 cup heavy whipping cream
- ½ cup confectioners' sugar

For the Shortcakes:

1. Preheat oven to 400°. Line a baking sheet with parchment paper. In a large bowl, whisk together flour, granulated sugar, rosemary, and salt. Using a pastry blender or 2 forks, cut butter into flour mixture until crumbly. Make a well in flour mixture; gradually add milk, stirring until mixture just comes together. Divide dough into 4 equal portions, and pat into 3-inch circles on prepared pan (see Note). Brush dough with cream.
2. Bake until golden brown, about 10 minutes. Let cool and cut in half horizontally.

For the Sauce:

1. In a large saucepan, bring 1 cup water, granulated sugar, and vinegar to a boil. Cook until syrupy, about 10 minutes. Add plums, apple, and zest; cook until fruit is tender, about 8 minutes.

For the Whipped Cream:

1. In a large bowl, beat cream with a mixer at medium-high speed until soft peaks form. Gradually add confectioners' sugar, beating until stiff peaks form.
2. To serve, spoon fruit and sauce over bottom half of shortcakes. Top with whipped cream, and cover with top halves.

NOTE: When forming shortcakes, make sure to pack the dough together so they won't crumble during cutting.

Buttermilk Biscuit Cinnamon Rolls

MAKES 8

If you love cinnamon rolls but are intimidated by yeast breads, these melt-in-your-mouth spirals are exactly what you've been looking for.

DOUGH

- **3 cups self-rising flour**
- **2 tablespoons granulated sugar**
- **½ cup cold unsalted butter, cut into pats**
- **1 cup plus 2 tablespoons cold whole buttermilk, divided**
- **3 tablespoons unsalted butter, softened**
- **¼ cup firmly packed light brown sugar**
- **¾ teaspoon ground cinnamon**
- **3 tablespoons unsalted butter, melted (optional)**

GLAZE

- **2 cups confectioners' sugar**
- **3 tablespoons whole buttermilk**
- **⅛ teaspoon kosher salt**

For the Dough:

1. Preheat oven to 450°. Lightly spray a 10-inch cast-iron skillet with cooking spray. In a large bowl, whisk together flour and granulated sugar. Using a pastry blender or 2 forks, cut cold butter into flour mixture until crumbly. Gradually stir in 1 cup buttermilk with a fork just until dry ingredients are moistened (add remaining 2 tablespoons buttermilk, if needed).

2. Turn out dough onto a lightly floured surface, and gently knead dough 5 times. Pat or gently roll dough to a 14x8-inch rectangle. Spread softened butter onto dough.

3. In a small bowl, stir together brown sugar and cinnamon; sprinkle onto buttered dough. Starting at one long side, roll up dough into a log. Cut roll into 8 (1¾-inch-thick) slices. Place slices cut side up in prepared pan.

4. Bake until golden brown, about 19 minutes. Brush melted butter onto rolls, if desired. Let cool on a wire rack for 10 minutes.

For the Glaze:

1. In a medium bowl, whisk together confectioners' sugar, buttermilk, and salt. For a thin glaze, drizzle onto warm rolls. For a thicker glaze, drizzle onto rolls after cooling for 30 to 45 minutes.

Biscuit Churros with Strawberry Sauce

MAKES 8 TO 10 SERVINGS

Doughnuts meet snickerdoodles in these beauties that are dunked in a fresh berry sauce.

2 cups chopped fresh strawberries
¾ cup plus 3 tablespoons sugar, divided
1 teaspoon fresh lemon juice
Vegetable oil, for frying
2 teaspoons ground cinnamon
3½ cups all-purpose baking mix*
1¼ cups hot water
1 teaspoon vanilla extract

1. In a small cast-iron Dutch oven, cook strawberries, 3 tablespoons sugar, and lemon juice over medium heat, stirring occasionally, until berries are soft and mixture is slightly thick, 12 to 15 minutes. Remove from heat, and mash with a potato masher until mixture is almost smooth. Let cool completely.

2. In a medium cast-iron Dutch oven, pour oil to a depth of 2 inches, and heat over medium heat until a deep-fry thermometer registers 350°.

3. In a shallow dish, whisk together ½ cup sugar and cinnamon. In a large bowl, whisk together baking mix and remaining ¼ cup sugar; whisk in 1¼ cups hot water and vanilla until a dough forms. Let stand for 5 minutes.

4. Spoon dough into a piping bag fitted with a large star tip. Working in batches, carefully pipe 4- to 5-inch-long pieces of dough into hot oil, cutting dough at piping tip with a knife or scissors between each piece.

5. Fry, turning frequently, until golden brown, 2 to 3 minutes. Let drain on paper towels. Dredge warm churros in cinnamon sugar to fully coat. Serve with strawberry sauce.

**We used Original Bisquick.*

Skillet Monkey Bread

MAKES 6 SERVINGS

This monkey bread makes a great, easy addition to any breakfast or brunch gathering. The toasted coconut on top adds a nice, sweet crunch.

1 (16.3-ounce) can refrigerated buttermilk biscuits
½ cup unsalted butter, melted
¾ cup sugar
2 teaspoons ground cinnamon
⅓ cup chopped pecans
⅓ cup sweetened flaked coconut
Cane syrup or maple syrup, to serve

1. Preheat oven to 350°. Spray a 10-inch ovenproof skillet with cooking spray.

2. Cut biscuits into quarters. In a small bowl, place melted butter. In another small bowl, stir together sugar and cinnamon. Working in batches, dip biscuit pieces in melted butter; roll in sugar mixture to coat. Place biscuit pieces in prepared pan. Sprinkle with pecans and coconut.

3. Bake until golden brown, about 25 minutes. Let cool for 15 minutes. Serve with cane syrup or maple syrup.

Apple-Pecan Monkey Bread

MAKES 10 TO 12 SERVINGS

With chunks of tart Granny Smith apple drenched in a buttery, cinnamon-laced caramel sauce, this monkey bread has all the flavors of apple pie, but it's so much simpler to prepare.

- **½ cup granulated sugar**
- **2 teaspoons pumpkin pie spice**
- **2 (16.3-ounce) cans refrigerated buttermilk biscuits**
- **1 apple, peeled, cored, and cubed**
- **½ cup chopped pecans**
- **½ cup unsalted butter**
- **⅓ cup firmly packed light brown sugar**
- **½ cup apple butter**

1. Preheat oven to 350°. Spray a 15-cup Bundt pan with baking spray with flour.

2. In a large bowl, stir together granulated sugar and pumpkin pie spice. Cut biscuits into quarters; toss in sugar mixture to coat. Layer coated biscuits, apple, and pecans in prepared pan.

3. In a small saucepan, heat butter and brown sugar over medium-high heat, stirring until sugar is dissolved, about 4 minutes. Remove from heat; stir in apple butter. Pour sugar mixture over layered biscuits, apple, and pecans in pan.

4. Bake until golden brown, about 35 minutes. Let cool in pan for 10 minutes. Invert onto a serving platter. Serve warm.

Persimmon and Almond Streusel Scones

MAKES 8

With crisp-tender chunks of sweet persimmon baked throughout, these warmly spiced scones are a cup of coffee's best friend.

DOUGH

- 3 cups all-purpose flour
- ¾ cup granulated sugar
- 1 tablespoon baking powder
- 2 teaspoons orange zest
- ¾ teaspoon kosher salt
- ½ teaspoon ground cardamom
- ¾ cup cold unsalted butter, grated
- 2 cups diced peeled firm Fuyu persimmon
- 1 cup whole milk
- 1 large egg
- ½ teaspoon almond extract

TOPPING

- ¼ cup all-purpose flour
- ¼ cup firmly packed light brown sugar
- ¼ cup sliced almonds
- 2 tablespoons unsalted butter, cubed and softened

Garnish: confectioners' sugar
Soft ripe persimmon, to serve

For the Dough:

1. Preheat oven to 400°. Spray a 10-inch cast-iron skillet with baking spray with flour. In a large bowl, whisk together flour, granulated sugar, baking powder, zest, salt, and cardamom; stir in cold butter. Freeze for 15 minutes. Stir in persimmon.

2. In a small bowl, whisk together milk, egg, and extract. Stir milk mixture into flour mixture just until dry ingredients are moistened. Turn out dough onto a heavily floured surface. Using well-floured hands, knead dough 5 to 10 times, about 1 minute. Shape dough into an 8-inch circle. Using a sharp knife, cut dough into 8 wedges. Gently place wedges in prepared pan, evenly spaced apart.

For the Topping:

1. In a small bowl, whisk together flour, brown sugar, and almonds. Add butter, pinching with fingers to incorporate. Squeeze mixture into large clumps. Sprinkle onto dough wedges. Freeze for 10 minutes.

2. Bake until golden brown, about 30 minutes. Let cool in pan on a wire rack for 5 minutes. Remove from pan, and let cool on a wire rack for 20 minutes. Garnish with confectioners' sugar, if desired. Serve scones with persimmon.

Chocolate Chip Banana Bread

MAKES 1 (8½X4½-INCH) LOAF

What makes sweet, moist banana bread even better? Add in chocolate morsels, of course!

1½ cups all-purpose flour
¾ cup sugar
1½ teaspoons baking powder
¼ teaspoon kosher salt
⅛ teaspoon ground cinnamon
⅛ teaspoon ground nutmeg
1 cup mashed ripe banana (about 2 medium bananas)
¼ cup vegetable oil
1 teaspoon vanilla extract
2 large eggs
¼ cup semisweet chocolate morsels
1 medium banana, halved lengthwise
1 tablespoon maple syrup

1. Preheat oven to 325°. Spray an 8½x4½-inch cast-iron loaf pan with baking spray with flour.

2. In a large bowl, whisk together flour, sugar, baking powder, salt, cinnamon, and nutmeg. In a medium bowl, combine mashed banana, oil, vanilla, and eggs. Add banana mixture to flour mixture, and beat with a mixer at low speed just until combined. Gently stir in chocolate morsels. Spoon batter into prepared pan. Place banana halves, cut side up, on top of batter. Brush banana halves with maple syrup.

3. Bake until a wooden pick inserted in center comes out clean, about 1 hour and 10 minutes, lightly covering with foil during last 10 minutes of baking to prevent excess browning, if necessary. Let cool in pan for 20 minutes. Run a knife around edges of bread. Remove from pan, and let cool completely on a wire rack.

Orange-Cardamom Loaves

MAKES 2 (8X4-INCH) LOAVES

The complex aroma of cardamom is so deliciously unique, and the spice pairs nicely with the floral citrus flavor of orange in this quick bread.

BREAD

3 cups all-purpose flour
1½ teaspoons kosher salt
1½ teaspoons baking powder
2½ cups granulated sugar
1½ cups whole milk
1 cup vegetable oil
3 large eggs
2 tablespoons orange zest
1½ teaspoons vanilla extract
¼ teaspoon ground cardamom

ORANGE GLAZE

2 cups confectioners' sugar
1 teaspoon orange zest
⅓ cup fresh orange juice

For the Bread:

1. Preheat oven to 350°. Spray 2 (8x4-inch) loaf pans with baking spray with flour. In a medium bowl, sift together flour, salt, and baking powder.

2. In a large bowl, beat granulated sugar, milk, oil, eggs, zest, vanilla, and cardamom with a mixer at medium speed until combined. Gradually add flour mixture to sugar mixture, beating until smooth. Divide batter between prepared pans.

3. Bake for 30 minutes. Loosely cover with foil, and bake until a wooden pick inserted in center comes out clean, about 30 minutes more.

4. Let cool in pans for 10 minutes. Remove from pans, and let cool completely on a wire rack.

For the Glaze:

1. In a medium bowl, whisk together confectioners' sugar and orange zest and juice until smooth. Drizzle glaze over cooled loaves.

Strawberry-Pistachio Bread

MAKES 1 (8½X4½-INCH) LOAF

This tasty quick bread gets a double dose of fruity flavor thanks to chopped fresh strawberries in the batter and sweet Strawberry Butter to serve.

BREAD

- 2 cups plus 2 teaspoons self-rising flour, divided
- ¾ cup plus 1 teaspoon granulated sugar, divided
- ⅓ cup finely chopped roasted salted pistachios
- ½ cup whole milk
- 2 large eggs
- 2 tablespoons unsalted butter, melted
- ½ teaspoon lemon zest
- 1 cup chopped fresh strawberries

Strawberry Butter (recipe follows), to serve

STRAWBERRY BUTTER

Makes about 1 cup

- ½ cup unsalted butter, softened
- ½ cup confectioners' sugar
- ½ cup coarsely mashed strawberries, drained
- ½ teaspoon lemon zest
- ¼ teaspoon vanilla extract

For the Bread:

1. Preheat oven to 350°. Lightly spray an 8½x4½-inch cast-iron loaf pan with baking spray with flour.
2. In a large bowl, whisk together 2 cups flour, ¾ cup granulated sugar, and pistachios; make a well in center of flour mixture.
3. In a small bowl, whisk together milk, eggs, melted butter, and lemon zest. Stir milk mixture into flour mixture just until combined.
4. In a small bowl, stir together strawberries and remaining 2 teaspoons flour; gently stir into batter. Spread batter into prepared pan.
5. Bake until a wooden pick inserted in center comes out clean, about 45 minutes. Sprinkle remaining 1 teaspoon granulated sugar onto hot bread. Let cool in pan on a wire rack for 10 minutes.
6. Run a knife around edges of pan. Remove bread from pan, and let cool on a wire rack for 30 minutes. Serve with Strawberry Butter.

For the Butter:

1. In a medium bowl, beat butter with a mixer at medium speed until creamy. Add confectioners' sugar, and beat until fluffy. Gradually add strawberries, beating until combined. Beat in lemon zest and vanilla. Serve immediately, or cover and refrigerate for up to 1 week. Let cold butter stand at room temperature until softened, about 20 minutes, before serving.

Sweet Potato Bread with Candied Pecans

MAKES 1 (9-INCH) LOAF

If you start dreaming about sweet potato bread in July, when it's way too hot to even say the word "oven" aloud, take heart. When temperatures do drop, this recipe will be waiting.

SWEET POTATO BREAD

2 cups all-purpose flour
1½ teaspoons ground cinnamon
½ teaspoon baking powder
½ teaspoon baking soda
½ teaspoon kosher salt
¼ teaspoon ground allspice
1¼ cups firmly packed light brown sugar
½ cup unsalted butter, melted
1 (15-ounce) can cut sweet potatoes in syrup,* drained and coarsely mashed
2 large eggs
1 teaspoon vanilla extract
½ teaspoon lemon zest
Cream Cheese Glaze (recipe follows)
Candied Pecans (recipe follows)

CREAM CHEESE GLAZE

⅔ cup confectioners' sugar
¼ cup cream cheese, softened
¼ teaspoon vanilla extract
1 tablespoon whole milk
1 to 2 tablespoons fresh lemon juice

CANDIED PECANS

Makes about 1½ cups

1 large egg white
¼ cup granulated sugar
1 teaspoon water
⅛ teaspoon kosher salt
⅛ teaspoon ground cinnamon
1½ cups pecan halves

For the Bread:

1. Preheat oven to 350°. Spray a 9-inch loaf pan with baking spray with flour.

2. In a large bowl, whisk together flour, cinnamon, baking powder, baking soda, salt, and allspice; make a well in center of flour mixture. In a medium bowl, whisk together brown sugar, melted butter, sweet potatoes, eggs, and vanilla. Pour over flour mixture, and beat with a mixer at low speed until combined. Stir in zest. Spoon batter into prepared pan, smoothing top.

3. Bake until a wooden pick inserted in center comes out clean, about 50 minutes. Let cool in pan for 10 minutes. Remove from pan, and let cool completely on a wire rack. Drizzle Cream Cheese Glaze over bread. Sprinkle with Candied Pecans.

For the Glaze:

1. In a small bowl, whisk together confectioners' sugar, cream cheese, vanilla, milk, and enough lemon juice until glaze reaches desired consistency.

For the Pecans:

1. Preheat oven to 250°. Line a rimmed baking sheet with foil, and spray with cooking spray.

2. In a medium bowl, whisk together egg white, granulated sugar, 1 teaspoon water, salt, and cinnamon until foamy. Add pecans; toss well. Using a slotted spoon, place pecan on prepared pan in an even layer. Bake until dry to the touch, about 1 hour, stirring occasionally. Let cool completely.

**We used Bruce's.*

Hummingbird Quick Bread

MAKES 1 (9-INCH) LOAF

One of the many things that quick breads have going for them is that, since they are technically bread and not cake, you can make the case that they're perfectly acceptable for breakfast.

BREAD

- 2 cups all-purpose flour
- 1 cup granulated sugar
- ½ cup sweetened flaked coconut, toasted
- ½ cup toasted pecans, chopped
- 1½ teaspoons baking powder
- 1 teaspoon ground cinnamon
- ½ teaspoon baking soda
- ½ teaspoon kosher salt
- ¼ teaspoon ground nutmeg
- ¼ teaspoon ground allspice
- ¼ teaspoon ground ginger
- 1 (8-ounce) can crushed pineapple, drained
- 1 cup mashed ripe banana (about 2 medium bananas)
- ¾ cup canola oil
- 2 large eggs
- 1 teaspoon vanilla extract
- Cream Cheese Glaze (recipe follows)
- Garnish: ground cinnamon

CREAM CHEESE GLAZE

- ⅔ cup confectioners' sugar
- ¼ cup cream cheese, softened
- ¼ teaspoon vanilla extract
- 1 tablespoon whole milk
- 1 to 2 tablespoons fresh lemon juice

For the Bread:

1. Preheat oven to 350°. Spray a 9-inch loaf pan with baking spray with flour.

2. In a large bowl, combine flour, granulated sugar, coconut, pecans, baking powder, cinnamon, baking soda, salt, nutmeg, allspice, and ginger. Make a well in center of flour mixture. In a medium bowl, combine pineapple, banana, oil, eggs, and vanilla. Add pineapple mixture to flour mixture, stirring just until moistened. Spoon into prepared pan.

3. Bake until a wooden pick inserted in center comes out clean, about 55 minutes. Let cool in pan for 10 minutes. Run a knife around edges of loaf; remove from pan, and let cool completely on a wire rack.

4. Drizzle with Cream Cheese Glaze. Garnish with cinnamon, if desired.

For the Glaze:

1. In a small bowl, whisk together confectioners' sugar, cream cheese, vanilla, milk, and enough lemon juice until glaze reaches desired consistency.

Molasses Walnut Banana Bread

MAKES 1 (8X4-INCH) LOAF

Molasses adds rich flavor and color to this crunchy-topped banana bread.

- ¼ cup whole buttermilk
- 1 teaspoon baking soda
- ½ cup unsalted butter, softened
- ¾ cup granulated sugar
- ⅓ cup molasses
- 2 large eggs
- 2¼ cups all-purpose flour
- ½ teaspoon kosher salt
- ½ teaspoon ground cinnamon
- ¼ teaspoon ground nutmeg
- 1½ cups mashed ripe banana (about 3 medium bananas)
- 1 teaspoon vanilla extract
- ½ cup chopped walnuts
- 1 large egg white
- 2 tablespoons firmly packed light brown sugar
- ¼ cup walnut halves
- Butter, to serve

1. Preheat oven to 325°. Spray bottom only of an 8x4-inch cast-iron loaf pan with baking spray with flour.

2. In a small bowl, stir together buttermilk and baking soda; let stand for 5 minutes. In a large bowl, beat butter, granulated sugar, and molasses with a mixer at medium speed until fluffy, 3 to 4 minutes, stopping to scrape sides of bowl. Add eggs, one at a time, beating well after each addition.

3. In a medium bowl, whisk together flour, salt, cinnamon, and nutmeg. With mixer on low speed, add flour mixture, buttermilk mixture, and banana to butter mixture, beating until combined. Beat in vanilla. Stir in chopped walnuts until combined. Spread batter into prepared pan.

4. In a small bowl, whisk egg white until frothy; stir in brown sugar. Pour onto batter, and sprinkle with walnut halves.

5. Bake until a wooden pick inserted in center comes out clean, about 1 hour and 45 minutes. Let cool in pan for 20 minutes. Remove from pan, and let cool completely on a wire rack. Serve with butter.

Recipe Index

BISCUITS

BREAD

COBBLERS

CORNBREAD

MISCELLANEOUS

MUFFINS

SCONES

SHORTCAKES